VOICES IN THE HALLS

Best of luck!

OTHER BOOKS BY DUNN NEUGEBAUER

*FUNNY CONVERSATIONS WITH GOD - AN
UNCALLED FOR DIALOGUE*

*ROCK BOTTOM, THEN UP AGAIN – AND OTHER
SPIRITUAL ESSAYS*

*WITS, WISDOMS, AND WONDERS FOR NAVIGATING
THIS THING CALLED LIFE*

MEDITATIONS FROM THE FINISH LINE

GRADUATION DAY

VOICES IN THE HALLS

AUTHOR OF *GRADUATION DAY* AND
MEDITATIONS FROM THE FINISH LINE

DUNN NEUGEBAUER

MOUNTAIN ARBOR
PRESS

**MOUNTAIN ARBOR
PRESS** *a Division of BookLogix*
Alpharetta, GA

ISBN: 978-1-6653-0670-6 – Paperback
eISBN: 978-1-6653-0671-3 – eBook

These ISBNs are the property of Mountain Arbor Press (a Division of BookLogix) for the express purpose of sales and distribution of this title. The content of this book is the property of the copyright holder only. Mountain Arbor Press does not hold any ownership of the content of this book and is not liable in any way for the materials contained within. The views and opinions expressed in this book are the property of the Author/Copyright holder, and do not necessarily reflect those of Mountain Arbor Press.

Library of Congress Control Number: 2023906618

Printed in the United States of America   0 4 1 8 2 3

♾This paper meets the requirements of ANSI/NISO Z39.48-1992 (Permanence of Paper)

Cover photo taken by Bill Ponder

The following essays are either true or based
on the truth, except for the one or two I completely
made up inside my head. Please know that zero malice
is intended towards anything or anyone in this book –
I'm a flawed soul but I genuinely hope everyone makes
a trillion dollars and ends up on Oprah.
And good luck with that.

CONTENTS

HIGH SCHOOL THEN – HIGH SCHOOL NOW

To be clear, I did graduate from high school, though it wasn't with the grace of the home run trot, nor a Peaches and Cream at Wimbledon type thing. Instead, it was more a driving in on two wheels, a hubcap flying off, another already gone, blood on the jeans, crud in the nose, hands clawed from trying to stay afloat.

We had so few people in my class back then, one day I actually thought I had a shot at being Valedictorian. I mean, I could handle war dates and English papers, though as far as math and foreign languages were concerned, to this very day I still don't know the difference.

The teacher's mouths moved in both cases, my C-minuses looked the same, so what me worry?

We were put in line by our "permanent records" and I'd love to see if my history teacher included that day we stole the globe and tore off the equator. Or when I complained that since the world was round, how could you have north, south, east, or west? And don't get me started about the time I memorized and recited George Carlin's 7 Words You Can't Say on Television.

The "lecture" I received over that one remains with me to this very day...

As for Latin, the teacher was sweet and passionate, but she was also 100 and drove about that fast leaving school. Years later, I understand why. And to think, poor Ken Brewer and I never understood why learning the phrase "puella est magnum" couldn't get us any dates.

Later, it was made clear. "The girl is large", after all, can be – and still is – a rather sensitive topic, and the fastest I ever moved – in any sport, season, or court – was ducking under a co-ed's left hook after delivering my Latin Brilliance.

We got whippings back then and, to be clear yet again, we deserved every smack, every ruler to the hand, and there was a notch in every belt loop that equaled the depth of our sins. I think there may have been a formula for that, maybe it was one of those things teachers plan at meetings, those gatherings I avoid to this very day.

My high school days, regardless, were proof that God did love us, because social media didn't exist, getting embarrassed with the touch of a button wouldn't happen until much later. You say pictures are worth 1000 words? Maybe, but I'm thankful to this day that would total about 10 million I can do without. Besides, maybe Shakespeare had it wrong, words really can hurt. (Key point: NEVER say that to your English teacher. NEVER!)

It's different now but it's the same. Boys still stare at pretty girls' back sides when they walk by. Fridays are better when your football team is good, and if you ever want to write a book about high school, just hang in the hallways for a little while.

Through it all - my papers back then were returned with enough red on them to resemble a scene from Jaws, my setting a record for getting the most kids into a 1969 Ford Falcon was a three-belt-loop-offense, learning creative ways to impress cheerleaders even though I quit football after 8th grade kept my mind sharp, and futile attempts at adding letters – it made high school sacred then, and I still feel that way now.

It's not Grease – mind you – you don't meet a hot blonde on the first day of school and dance on top of cars the whole time. And Human Psychology remains the thing you learn best.

In closing, I didn't cry at my graduation, though to this day a tear drops every spring for our kids. It's like a cumulative exam, if you will, each class creates new memories while at the same time keeps stirring up the old ones. It's a head rush times 12, making me wish I'd did more, meant more, loved more, wrote more. My thoughts rush at me so fast I'm often reciting them to a nearby tree – not kidding but at least I don't get slapped that way - though I did irritate a rather large hornet's nest once.

What can I tell you – a writer's life doesn't always appear to be a sane thing – at least in my case it doesn't. There's no appointed game time – when the words come you take the shortest distance between two points and you find a pen or pencil, pad, or computer. Or if you're old enough, a typewriter.

Enough said, but with all that, I graduate without honors – again – but you'll never hear me complain. And I'm grateful also that with all I refused to learn back then, I'm learning that and then some now.

Walking hallways without a belt,

Enjoy your school year…

AN UNUSUAL START TO A BOOK

I forgot the page where the author is supposed to thank people, though, in all my life I've rarely read this part. After all, I have no idea who these people are and I have other things to care about. Seriously, do I want to read that John T. Smith edited this, or Suzie Ormeister gave me the idea? My computer is putting a red line under Ormeister as I write this, so even machinery could care less.

With that said, I'm going to do it this way: Since I'm a slow starter and have trouble warming up, I'm going to cut to the chase. Or to the halls rather, since that's in the title of this book.

The beginning of a new school year is similar to New Year's resolutions. You start strong, fresh off the charger, renewed. You're going to conquer the world though you're probably not going to change a thing in trying to do it. You may not write any of it down, so later you'll deny it was your goal.

Still, the energy is, or shall I say, was good.

So, I captured it. Here's some random goals before the first bell even rang.

- School? I just want to bowl a 300!
- I want shorter panini lines! The toaster was fried before I got up front last year!
- Just help me remember how to tie a tie on chapel day. Then again, maybe I'll steal my dad's clip-on again.
- I just want to learn how to fly a plane and put out fires. Why do I have to take Latin again to get to do that?

- To make it to the bathroom this year if I catch the stomach bug again.
- To not fall out of my desk. How did that happen anyway?
- Not to drop the baton on the relays. One of my teammates never talked to me after that. Then again, he graduated so who cares?
- To make the Headmaster's List...but this time the positive one.
- I'm making a deal with God on passing math. Maybe I should share this with my teacher.
- Glasses! I just need new glasses! It's hard to make good grades when you can't see what the teacher's putting on the Smart Board.
- To get accepted to a college...in a land far, far, away.
- To not lead the junior class in demerits and detentions. Then again, to not be a junior at all when this school year ends.
- I just hope my mother doesn't make me speak in chapel again. Then again, I did so bad last year I probably won't get asked back.
- To go the whole year and not even know who's on the Honor Council.
- To not fall asleep in Spanish!
- I want to break 20 minutes in the 5K!
- Ten homers, .400 average, region title.
- Is it too early to ask someone to prom? No? Too needy?
- To remember to tuck my shirttail in. Why is that so hard?
- To lip sync in chapel. After all, the other kids have ears, too.

- Get some sleep, maybe? Before 2:00 a.m. this year? How does it get so late so quick anyway?
- Make varsity even if I don't get to play. At least I can practice against better people.
- What does any boy want – to win his Fantasy Football league of course.
- To win my bet on who's going to get Homecoming king and queen. I already know.
- To not get blamed for belching in class again. I'm not going to tell who it really was last year, but his initials are Ken Thomas.
- Get these (bleeping) senior essays off to colleges.
- To not lead my hoops' squad in charges taken. Is there even a stat for that?
- To not have my shot blocked into the eighth row again. Boy, dad was so proud…
- Don't fall in love…just enjoy the school year.
- I want to at least wait until I'm a sophomore before senioritis sets in. That's late enough, right?
- I just want a rule where cross country meets start later on a Saturday. Dunkin Donuts isn't even open we're up so early.
- My goal? There are 180 of them and I'm counting each day until this is over.
- To not get slapped by a cheerleader. Again.
- More chicken tender days and the speed to get to the front of the line first.
- Learn how to play singles since my doubles partner graduated.
- C's and above, babe, just C's and above.

There it is…and more. Taught to color between the lines, don't move out of my box, and write only in #2 pencils, I've become attached to chaos – as long as it means well.

And, if you want a normal acknowledgement page, I'd like to thank my mother. After all, she let me be a brat, but she made sure I meant well. And now that I've followed in her footsteps and have walked halls for years, my next job will be to put up a psychiatry practice, with the sign on my door reading:

The Shrink Who Needs a Shrink!
"After all, how else would I know?"

Okay, on with the book. It's random, the socks don't match, the words don't rhyme, and it's plaids mixed with solids.

Maybe that's high school. And maybe that's me.

God Bless,

Dunn
Author, Coach, Nice but Messed up Guy

THE. FIRST. DAY. OF. SCHOOL

America used to be baseball, hot dogs, apple pie, and Chevrolet. Now it's become ear buds, cellphones, a divisive country, and social media. Personally, I prefer my mom's apple pie, but she died, so here I am.

Working carpool.

And I'm trying to tell drivers that the car will go off road if you're texting, it won't move until you put your foot on the gas (it's next to the brake last I checked), and when humans are crossing the street, for Heaven's sakes, STOP! Also, if that guy is 16 and he's driving, then I'm going to have to ask for a raise for doing this.

Seriously!

After all, a grandmother almost ended my life one day out here. She meant well – she was just waving to her overloaded, stuffed to the gills, backpack, sweetheart - but in all due respect to her young one, I almost bought it.

Anyway, there's music playing out here since it's the first day, perhaps trying to create a rhythm to all this. The lyrics are telling me this is going to be the best day of my life, yet after the first 20 minutes out here, the day better get better in a hurry if that's the case.

After all, each parent must get a picture of their offspring of The First Day of School. They love it as much as the kids hate it, and you can see it in the forced, get me out of here grin on the youth's faces. It is what it is, but even though I'm not a parent, it might not be the best day when the kid prefers the rigor of the classroom over posing for a picture.

I smile, briefly thanking my ex for not letting us reproduce. Then again, how was that possible with me on the couch, another three-rose offense debt unpaid, but a good sitcom on TV so I'd try again tomorrow?

Maybe I should've known – you never know when you'll run out of tomorrows. Maybe they'll teach that here. Or somewhere. Regardless, a couch to this day represents freedom, sleeping in jeans if I want, and loving the art of renting 571 kids, then going home.

Still, my karmic debt for avoiding that responsibility is meeting all 571 of them, translating the randomness of their minds if possible, and loving trying to stay sane while trying to love each and every one of them.

I was an academic incompetent, but God told me that love was the only thing that lasted, though I'd counter that Debbie Sharpley's legs in that Prom dress back in 1977 ran a close second.

Then again, I'm not really sure God approves of me sometimes.

And maybe that's why I'm working carpool instead of Debbie, dodging Broncos and Pathfinders instead of curing cancer, and trying to believe this really will be the best day of my life.

In seriousness, though, I appreciate God's sense of humor, and I have trouble with people who don't. After all, we live in a world where some guy thought eating a bat was a good idea, people beating each other up in cages makes millions, and yet poor teachers who pour their souls into making sense of things have to work in peach sheds over the summer and tutor on the side just to make ends meet.

I used to not be a teacher's pet because I didn't deserve it. Today, I see and hear what they do every day and I still don't. Yet I'm a fan. And though not possessing the wisdom of any subject, the guts to face 20 or so for five hours a day, or enough oil in my lamp to plan for day's ahead, I can still support.

Thus me. Here. Carpool. With horns, loud music, and selfies, and chattering. And without my Advil.

It's okay, though, as if I'm thrown out on my non-academic butt, at least I have my couch. My freedom. And the choice to change the station when that horrible music comes on.

So, Happy First Day of School. And smile knowing it doesn't matter if you're having a good hair day or not. Your mother will find it priceless – and your picture will be on her fridge before the news at noon.

Now cars get out of here. No matter how smart you are, the line will back up if you're sitting there texting, and I'm going to class regardless.

After all, it's a new year. And I'm curious if this is going to be the best day – and/or the best year - of my life.

THE TRANSITION

The problem with our world isn't pollution, the ozone layer, politics, or traffic, but instead the alarm clock.

Before I explain, I get that we don't live in a society that feels sorry for private school kids. After all, the word on the street is their bathroomings smell like lilly water *, their noses are higher in the air than all nine planets (or is it eight? Did Pluto ever get reinstated), and they drive to school in Porsche's.

Personally, I have to park my Honda in the "These people just work here," lot, with no charge except risking our lives crossing Mt. Vernon, and our eternal health is at the hands of a hired security guard who's wondering how he drew this gig.

And maybe his alarm clock's loud as well. How would he know?

My point is the differential – as one minute the kid is approaching a British bombshell on the beach, the next there's a noise so loud that's eight octaves higher than middle C and whales are beaching themselves as far away as Miami.

If I ever retire, I'm going to go into business as an alarm clock salesman as I'm sure more than a few are broken over the course of a year. Business will be booming! Still, I won't be very popular – sort of like the dentist or that guy that checks you for a hernia, but we really don't have to discuss that hernia-checking thing...

Anyway, change happens. But going from bombshells to algebra in one short hour can cause a bit of derangement, and I have found in my Studies of Fellow Humans that ones who never learn to adapt to the above noise often wind up parking trucks at strip joints or handing out toilettes in swanky restaurant bathrooms.

But, as usual, I digress.

Curious about this, I had to march through the hallways in the early days (subs aren't too busy in the first week) and I entertained the question of "The Art of Adjusting" to our now overloaded youth who are already cramming their skulls with theorems, facts, and war dates.

Here are some of the replies:

- Oh yeah, it's a transition all right. In fact, it sorta blows.
- How many days before Thanksgiving break again?
- From staring at breasts to taking tests...you do the math...
- Math? Did that guy just mention math? Good lord I think we have a quiz...Or maybe that's French?
- I cried myself to sleep.
- I've Googled self-hypnosis – am curious about how to look people in the eye, nod my head at appropriate times, and still not have a clue what they're talking about.
- I'm either going to have to become spiritual or start a rock band. Can you do both?
- I shaved my head. Wait, what was the question again?
- It's all about breaking it down into segments. How long until break? Lunch? Free period? The last bell? If you don't do that you'll end up in the counselor's office before Labor Day.
- Counselor's office? Where is that by the way?
- My solution was to sit next to the hot girls and

return to my dream. Wouldn't you know it – my first two classes were all guys.

- I'm going to have to take up a new hobby! Actually, when will I have time to do that?
- How many absences do we get?
- I turn the music up louder in my ear buds.
- One minute I'm fishing, the next I'm being caught.
- I lost my organizer/planner thingie so you're going to have to ask somebody else.
- (One kid just stared – his eyes looked through me to parts unknown. A smart man only in emergencies, I got the hell out of his way.)
- Sorry, I forgot the question already but will you help me with my college entrance essay? It has to be 650 words or less.
- I'm not sure how to transition since they wouldn't let me take four art classes, two free periods, and lunch. Wow, this is a cold world!
- Transition? Into this? Not sure but what block is this? Isn't this M? And why is that one always before lunch?

It just goes on like that, whatever "that" is. Still, I quit asking since I'd already reached the proverbial word count on this essay. In fact, I'm getting the email from the boss right now.

The story is late, she says. Of course, it is.

After all, I'm running behind today because i forgot to set my alarm…

Actually, I'm not real sure what lilly water is, or if it even exists. Still, like John Belushi in Animal House, I was on a roll. Or so I thought…

DISSECTING A FROG
(Adolescent Flashback)

I wasn't really sure if it was the smell or the actual looks of the glazed-up frog that made me want to barf. Then again, barf doesn't care – it just starts at your navel, breaks traffic laws getting past your heart, and before you know it, you're staring at your earlier lunch now resting on Kenny Watkins' high tops.

My first thought, before the actual embarrassment set in was, "Cool shoes! I wonder if they'll let us order those for basketball season?"

Still, it was in a science class that I had to somehow pass where I learned those teachers could be stubborn, too. I already knew coaches were – I'd done enough suicides on a basketball court to need more than a pair of shoes already.

But I'm doing now what I did back in lab that day – I'm avoiding the approach of the frog. With a knife in my hand. With a lab partner – female – who's already hiding her nose under her goggles. (Why she needed goggles, I wasn't really sure. Then again, there's a lot I still don't know about females, so let's move on.)

Anyway, there's the frog. And me with the knife. My partner is leaning in, as if this is going to help. The teacher is in arm-folding if-you-don't-hurry-you'll-get-an-F position. And glancing at the clock does me no good, it actually seems to be going backwards.

No way out.

Blessed with the steady hands of an alcoholic in need of his first drink, Dr. Dunn stood over the frog. Hmm, do I name him? No, naming him makes it more personal. Do I stab him first to make sure he's dead? No, I can assure you, that is one dead frog sitting in this pan. Why this frog and who caught him? And did he sign that organ donor thing that's on the back of driver's licenses?

"We're waiting." Oh, that teacher again. Sounded just like that basketball referee that night when he'd handed me the ball and was waiting on my free throw.

I missed, by the way – the free throw, not the frog.

Because my thinking was this: why make little bitty incisions and make it last forever, when I could just wail on the thing and get it done quickly? I started laughing, because I thought of that Name That Tune game, the one where you had to say how few notes you could identify the song.

"I can flog this frog in three strokes!" See, I thought that was funny! Problem was the teacher and my partner didn't agree. And we didn't live in a world where you got extra points for smartassery, and I know that isn't a word. (Right click, add to dictionary – now it is!)

Okay, I'm back – it's Dr. Dunn, in the Lab Room, with the knife. Ah, a reference from Clue, though that board game hadn't been invented yet. Wow, instead of being dumb, was I actually ahead of my time?

Doubtful. And I sure didn't have the grades to back that up.

In moving on (finally), my knife entered the jellied up, nasty, greasy, frog. It was sort of like cutting a steak, but with a different smell. And I doubt I could put A1 sauce on a dead frog.

Getting the hang of it – the third time's the charm, but the first time's the alarm (Wow, a saying!), I zigged, zagged, swiped, swooped, slashed, and gashed, gripped and ripped that poor, disgusting, former creature.

I'd gone into sort of a fugue state, probably because there was no other way.

My lab partner was shocked – what had gotten into me? The teacher stepped in to view my "work." The former marinated frog now resembled a Georgia road map so exact, it even had places like Social Circle, Eatonton, Farmington, and Bishop on there.

My partner took off her goggles. The teacher's expression can't be expressed, not in words anyway. And with that, he turned and walked out of the room.

Rumor has it, he went to the bathroom to puke.

Class dismissed.

THE NOTE

To be truthful, his mother really did make him do it.

And to be clear, he begged and pleaded with her not to make him run cross country. Those kids got up too early on Saturday's, puked a lot, hung together in skinny, angular packs, wore funny looking boots when injured, and often talked in numbers.

And besides, he was bad at math.

Mom struck him a deal. "Here's a note. It's signed. All you have to do is sign your half, date it, and you can turn it in to the coach any day, any time you wish. If you sign it and quit, I will ask NO questions, will give you no grief, and you'll get no extra chores. Got it?"

What could he say? When you're 15 and your mother tells you something, you have to "get it." Still, on that first morning, when the alarm fired at some God awful time, he cussed her name and the judge that sentenced him to be with her instead of his dad. Envied so badly his friends, who were now choosing between the beach or the ocean, a three or a four-iron.

Or maybe they were smart and were asleep.

He sat on the bleachers listening to three skinny adults. Ground rules. Water bottles. Safety first. Health forms. All but he seemed to know the language, as the group nodded their heads at appropriate times, seemed to know when to quit giggling. He was nervous, so for his security blanket, he reached inside his pocket and put his hand around the note.

It felt warm. Safe. Stationary. Calmed his nerves.

When they hit the track, he fell in with his assigned group. It was a mile warmup, and he vaguely knew a couple of the guys in his pack. His goal was to avoid embarrassment, hope his joints and muscles didn't speak louder than the conversation, and to keep up best he could.

After all, it was bad enough not being a football jock. Dang if he was going to fail at something that wasn't even a real sport.

Moving on, he did what decently good boys do – he changed classes, ogled the older girls, took lunch at the nerd table, made it through monotoned lectures. And after school, he'd lace them up and head off for practice.

The two-week report was that he was sore and had JV written all over every fiber of his body. It was hot out. Often running after school was a lot, but at least the #4 girl was pretty hot, and it was keeping him away from his cellphone and his video games. Still, in true angst of the boy that he was, he couldn't even keep up with girl #4, so he just dropped his head, panted and pouted and pounded his way through practices.

His saving grace was, he still hadn't puked. And all the while, his "get out of jail free" card rustled around in his pocket.

As the races started, he knew this sport wasn't his thing, but it had become a habit. His coach put him in the first JV race, he finished and not last – even beat one of the older boys. That wasn't what gave him a bit of a thrill, but instead it was this:

Some internet race site had his name listed, with his school and his time. His time wasn't good, mind you – he started from the bottom when looking for himself – but there it was. Wow. If nothing else, he was an official stat in his state.

Midseason approached. Fall was here though someone forgot to tell Mother Nature, who insisted on flaunting more summer and pushing back the fall. His former pain was now a part of his life, perhaps a bit of a medal of honor. He had his group, his pack. His number – still not good – kept getting better. He even had a nickname.

Okay, the nickname was nothing to read into – it was "Chucklehead." The reason was his name was Chuck and he fell down one day and hit his head. Simple. Still, he knew enough to know that that was called trail diving. Like turning the corner in French class, he was picking up the language, learning the rhythms, catching on.

And on the social side of things, he still hadn't asked Hot #4 out, but he could least now catch her at practice. She even smiled the other day, told him "Good job" as he temporarily jogged beside her. He noticed runners said that a lot, "Good job."

Really? How did they know? He quit thinking, smiled back, mumbled something, then jogged away.

In getting to the end, maybe it was two weeks before region, he's still not sure. And unfortunately, this doesn't have the made for Hollywood ending. This wasn't Rocky calling for Adrian with blood all over his face, nor was the Road Queen Family Truckster making it to Wally World. As for an article, it'd be nothing to make Running World or to send to that Roy Benson fellow at Running Times.

If he had to label it, it was perhaps a synchronicity that seemed to develop out of all this chaos, this thing he now knew and respected, this thing he argued about the other day. No, he wasn't good, but cross country was indeed, a sport. He almost wanted to fight about it but then, he remembered how skinny he was, though now at least chiseled and angled a bit.

Anyway, the girls were in their starting box, sprinting out, trotting back, sprinting out, trotting back. On about the fourth time, he watched while the girls, almost as if approaching some invisible altar, came together – all seven – then clasped together as one.

They even bowed their heads. Did they talk? He didn't know, and maybe that was a good thing. After all, words would seem to…he didn't know …mess this up somehow. Anyway, they stayed like that for a few seconds. Seven girls. One huddle. One team. One race.

Finally, they unlatched, trotted to the box, got ready to go. He was mesmerized by this, and, to this day, he can't put his finger on why.

As for him, he jogged back to the tent to get ready for his own event. True, the finish line tape would be scattered, tattered, smushed, and crushed by the time he got there. Still, he had a number in his head, a time to beat.

And as he took off his sweats, something fell to the ground. Confused, he picked it up, unfolded it, remembered what it was. It was a contract, signed by his mother. A blank line was by his name, the date also left untouched, waiting for his quitting hand.

As if on cue, his mother walked up, she was 15 yards away and counting.

"Chucklehead! Let's go, we're warming up!" It was his teammates.

"One second guys."

And with that, he trotted away from his teammates over to his mother. He kissed her on the cheek, but before joining his teammates, he handed her a note, an unsigned note. She looked at it, inspected it as only a mother can.

And as she watched her son run off to join in his teammate's huddle, a tear slowly dropped out of her eye.

ADVICE FOR HIGH SCHOOL GRADUATES

- Be proactive – unless you're concocting a stink bomb or planning a panty raid.
- Call your mom – she worries, and she probably has good reasons for doing so.
- Choose a college that's far enough away to be far enough away, yet close enough where you can drive home, get your laundry done, and ask mom or dad for more money
- Be careful when looking at a female's name tag. She might think you're getting fresh. (Reporting this for a friend, of course).
- Take naps. Two hours of sleep over a three day period is NEVER acceptable.
- Still, and on the other hand, pull an all-nighter. Think Bourbon Street if you will, everybody should do it at least once.
- If the lowest grade the professor gives is a "C", then don't drop the class! And thank you Dr. McKenzie after all these years and forgive me for never knowing what determinism is or was.
- If you get off to a bad start and set you bar low, don't give up. After all, even sports teams give "Most Improved" awards.
- Never play on an intramural football team with people who never got to play high school sports. They'll treat every game like it's the Super Bowl and the simple fact is, it's not.
- Never throw up at the "Welcome New Students" dance. They might strip away the above name tag and you might not be welcome any more. (Seriously,

reporting that for someone who wasn't there long enough for me to learn his name.)

- Be nice – in victory or defeat, whether getting the girl or getting dumped. Rejection is projection and, if you win, act like you do it all the time and you're used to it.
- Never spike the Hawaiian Punch on a tennis road trip. Poor Joel never knew what hit him. (But man was he funny!)
- Go with an open mind. I went "knowing" that the only rock group was the Beatles, and the only sports team was the Bulldogs. I left knowing I was wrong in both cases.
- Never jump off cliffs in Blue Hole, Alabama. Think about it – jumping off cliffs is pretty dumb anyway.
- Be nice. Live by the Golden Rule. Lead with love and all else will follow. Pick one or any of those – they all work.
- Open the doors for women, pay for their dinner on dates, and treat them with respect. And don't be surprised if rumors fly when you walk a drunk one to the door. Just take the credit you don't deserve and move on.
- Never try to wrestle with or dwell on a problem. Just ask God for the solution and go do something else. After all, Einstein wasn't wrong when he said that you can't solve a problem with the same mind that created it. If the problem's too bad, take a nap.
- But don't fall asleep in accounting class. Some teachers get REALLY mad about that.
- Never high five the hitter on the volleyball team. You may lose your arm.

- When in doubt, practice and learn the art of shutting the hell up.
- Unless you're working carpool and your friend is about to get hit by a Pathfinder.
- Never relieve yourself behind the R.A.'s trailer. Those people tend to have longer memories than women and elephants combined.
- If a very large man with tattoos, green teeth, and with a motorcycle out back wants to fight you, don't. After all, staying alive trumps both being right and wrong.
- Don't stare at your cellphone. I promise you, in college, there are a lot better things to stare at.
- And finally, don't play cornerback wearing slippers, never go to class wearing Susan's overalls, and never put your underwear in the Time Capsule. You'll never hear the end of any of these!

Bon voyage!

A LEGACY FOR HIS DAD

Maybe your beginning of becoming whole is when you start living for someone that's gone.

Okay, maybe Tommy wasn't quite able to put things in that sort of perspective, in fact the only thing he knew on this night was that he was about to play in his last football game and, like all the other games before him, he simply and silently pulled out a magic marker and wrote #13 on his helmet.

He was #54, for the record, but he wasn't a noticeable kid so who would notice? In fact, if you looked up his stats you probably wouldn't find any, and if you looked on opposing scouting reports you wouldn't find his name at all.

Still, he did what he did – and scribbling that number in honor of his fallen dad made things...okay somehow. He remembered the day they'd given him #54, he'd gone home mad because he wanted dad's number.

Dad, in turn, got mad because he was mad, telling him to take his own number, start his own thing, make future generations want to wear his jersey.

That hadn't exactly happened. Division I scouts, or for that matter Division II or III, didn't know or care he existed. He'd probably end up at a small in-state college, maybe a JUCO and work his way through things – whatever all these things were.

He'd gone through games and life wishing he could make his dad proud, he really did, and perhaps that's what often made things worse. First, the result. Then, the comparison.

Regardless, and in moving on, the fourth quarter rolled around with his team behind as usual. The coach called his name and, with the nerves that always got to the field a few steps before he did, Tommy took his place on the defensive line.

This isn't a hero tale, for the record, as Tommy got plowed on the first two plays but still, on the game's last play and on the last one of his football life, it was perhaps fitting that he assisted on a tackle.

As for the aftermath, no one carried him off the field, it was just another play, another day, and Tommy did what he always did – he congratulated his teammates on giving it a good try, hugging the tear-felt people in the huddle after a crazy and losing season. Wishing people well. Thanks for the opportunity. All that.

When the hugs had ended and the coach's attempt at making sense of all this almost made sense, Tommy walked away in private. He was funny that way and, in spite of trying to fit in in so many ways, this was a habit he'd keep.

He thought of his dad, and would he be proud of him? He hadn't done much, didn't leave his jersey encased in a frame on a gym wall. There was no legacy here. But then again...wait a minute.

Something got through inside his skull...exactly this:

Who was to say what leaving a legacy meant anyway. Being a good teammate, showing up every day, and helping the man next to you wasn't so bad, right? In fact, in a crazy sort of way, maybe this was a great kind of legacy – silent, proper behavior. Helping others. Serving. Assisting.

Why did other people always have to know?

It was that thought that moved him off into the night; that thought that made sense, forced tears flowing from his face as he walked off the field.

So, with that, Tommy - making no effort to show his emotion - took off his helmet and pointed up to the sky...

THE P.E. CLASS
(Adolescent flashback)

Perhaps there was a certain nobility in getting hit square in the face with a dodgeball at 8:06 on a Monday morning, but as you lay sprawled on the gym floor in front of the coach and all your peers, you were yet to be very clear on what it was.

At least you were awake – sort of – and since you were too young to be slurping coffee like the rest of the world and your morning dose of Tang didn't do it, a dodgeball slung at you at high speed, from the quarterback no less, did the job just fine.

Thinking back, growing up was a case study in the Art of Getting Hit in the Face in general. Two years prior, Sammy Powers swing full tilt at a playground curveball and connected full force – with your head.

The ball never moved though you were halfway between home and first. Still, it's funny the things you remember. You were convinced you were dying, so now Mark would have a private room at home and at least you wouldn't have to walk and feed the dog anymore.

You made a note of your sins vs. your confessions, and you'd started life okay but once you found out that girls' bodies had curves to them and curfews were made to be broken, you were waffling about which way you'd get sent.

Then the first black eye – you'd seen people with black eyes, though you never knew it swelled up like a grapefruit first. Getting elbowed in the face playing gym hockey, whatever that was provided another great memory, and taking a solid right hook from Betsy Sale when telling her you didn't think the Atlanta Flames would make the playoffs was yet another.

Later in life a car wreck and 150 stitches in your face was perhaps an exclamation point, a reminder of the things life can throw at you.

But back to P.E. class, which always began with hope upon hope not to be on the "skins" side of things, as some of your classmates seemed to be born with facial and chest hair, and many seemed to be tanned even in the throes of February.

As for you, you'd grow your first chest hair later in life – as a 43-year-old to be exact.

It was that and that alone that led to the above dodgeball-to-face incident speaking of, as being on the skins team you had both arms crossed over your body, hiding all it could. After all, wasn't it your very own P.E. teacher that earlier in the year said, "Dunn, if I had a body like that, I'd hide it."

So, you were – trying to anyway. And all you got was a dodgeball to the skull and a trip to the nurse's office.

Looking back, adolescent life was and is confusing. Who to believe? What's right? Wrong? How to proceed? And attention deficit disorder medicine was yet to be created on top of that.

Perhaps what added to the puzzlement was years earlier, also in the dreaded world of P.E., while on the Lower School playground.

Your class was playing Red Rover, Red Rover but your bastard classmates would never call you right over. Taught that very morning that honesty was the best policy, you got out of line and told Coach Smith – face to face - that this particular game was very boring.

Not to say that you ran laps, though later in life you'd

become a distance runner, so perhaps you have him to thank. And Red Rover. And honesty.

Looking at it all, P.E. class seemed to be a constant reminder that if you weren't very good at this game, don't fret because the coach would introduce you to another one you weren't so hot at as well. Four squares. Kick ball. Pick-up basketball. Tag. Relay races. That crazy game where you hop along while in a burlap sack.

And where did they get all those sacks and why?

Present day, your face healed though your facial receiving's of the past often have you talking to tree branches or perhaps a library book. Fortunately, you have Tourette's, so you can blame some of it on that.

Regardless, things never seemed to have gotten better when comparing your present self to all those P.E. days. Sure, you have four chest hairs now, you shave twice and week and you're only 62-years-old, so perhaps there's hope.

Still, you smile. After all, you've your own private room now, your ex took the dogs, and you'd earlier in life changed your major your last semester of college.

Think about it, you had actually trained to become a P.E. teacher.

Jesus wept.

THE ART OF INTERVIEWING THREE CHEERLEADERS AT THE SAME TIME...

Before I start, let me point something out. Whenever you, as a sub or a teacher, tell the students that if they don't finish this particular assignment, then what's left will be for homework, what the kids actually hear is, "We can screw off for the rest of the class because this isn't due until tomorrow!" I know this because, as a veteran, I now think and speak in High School, not yet declared an official language though I hope soon it will be.

Another point to be made is that I get bored as well, so once I read this soon-to-be-ignored part of the lesson plan, my eyes scan the audience for potential stories, interviews, conversations. We might as well make use of the time, right?

With that said, my eyes landed on three cheerleaders, just off of tryout week. I know this not because I know their schedule, but because there is funk still on their faces from staying up too late every day recently. One of them, in fact, though scribbling something in her notebook, is having trouble keeping her head off the desk – a drool-infested nap is probably soon in her future.

In moving forward, I called all three to my desk, at once – an unofficial "meeting" if you will – and I inquired about last week.

Now, one more point before I go on. Since all three talked at once, I have NO idea who said what. Just know that words came out at 750 words per minute with gusts up to 1250. Sometimes kids wait for others to quit talking, sometimes they don't. As an adult, there's more of a filter so you sift and sort often before talking. Not so as an adolescent.

As I said, I speak high school.

So, below is an incredibly rough translation of what was said, and I'll attribute it to the same mouth, since they were all moving at the same time anyway. Let's move on…and wish me luck.

"It was SOOOOO stressful."

"Oh my God!'

"Nerve-racking!"

"It was exciting. No, it was stressful. No, it was…well…both of those and more."

"Emotional, that's what it was! Will I make it? Will she make it? Who will make it?"

"The most I slept in one night was three hours. Maybe four."

"It reminded me of cheer camp. One day a roach got on my toothbrush. I threw it away and started crying."

"I know, right? I couldn't sleep because I was scared one would drop down on my head!"

"Seriously, you get the routine on Sunday, around noon or so, and then your whole week is about getting behind in all your classes because you're learning dances and stuff. Hey, what was that dance we did freshmen year?"

(The talk pauses while they try to remember. They're dancing now, discussing just what the moves were. Now, in the overall scheme of things, it really doesn't make a rat's behind what they were, but this seems REALLY important to them right now. So, they dance. Think Tik Tok with nobody filming.)

"We have 6:30 a.m. workouts Tuesday through Thursday. You're practicing, trying to learn and keep up with all the stuff. And go to school."

"And then there's Friday!"

"What happens on Friday." You pat yourself on the back for finding room to throw in some syllables of your own.

"At around 9:30-ish, if you don't make it, you get an email. So, you're checking your phone and checking your phone, hoping for an email that you don't get. Still, what if you get it and don't make it while your good friend does. Or the other way around?"

"And if you don't get it, you still don't know whether you got the sport or sports you wanted, you know? Did I get football, basketball, or both? Do I want both? I mean, basketball season goes FOREVER! But still, I like being cheerleader."

"Regardless, after all that, you're like really tired. (All three chime in as if they've practiced at this point) ... "You are SOOOO tired. Exhausted. Useless. So ready for bed. Even though it's Friday, you set the alarm for Sunday."

The bell rings, probably a good thing. After all, your ears are starting to hurt. They walk away, still discussing those freshman year moves. Out the door they go, still yakking, our youth filled with 28 hours of energy even though there's only 24 in a day.

As for you, you're now SOOOO tired.

And to think, running practice remains…

Jesus wept…

A RED SKY OVER MT. VERNON MORNING

It's funny how things work...

Raised with a grandfather for a Baptist preacher and a life that consisted of church, Bible school, and stories you had trouble believing regarding fishes and loaves, parted seas, burning bushes, and sins etched on tablets, you'd never had any real evidence of this God being that was supposed to keep you out of ...well...more burning.

Still, as you stand here on this September morning, a carpool vest announcing that you do have a purpose in life, and with the morning traffic not quite picked up yet, you happen to turn and face east.

And there it was: A red sky over Mt. Vernon Highway, the sun partially peeking out, as if not quite awake itself, though it's glow already casting a spell over your eyes that still hadn't gotten past the morning glaze. You could see the rays – like arms – peacefully pointing out in all directions – and the result was postcard perfect.

Red. Orange. Yellow. White. All blending together as if sending a message of peace, protecting you if you will. You just stand there, looking up. Mesmerized. In fact, if you were a photographer, you'd be there complete with tripod and a binocular-powered lens.

Yeah, you think. You're very sure no dude could've come up with this. Good morning, God. Glad to finally meet you. Seeing, as well as feeling, is believing.

Minutes later, there comes one. She's a junior, our softball pitcher, still wearing her softball glove for what-ever reason, and she's looking like most high school kids do – places to go, people to see, and if you speak, speak fast. After all, there will be more than plenty of lectures for later.

Not sure why the glove, though maybe she's expecting a ground ball to come out of Parking Space #24.

"Did you see that game yesterday," she asks almost angrily.

"Some of it," you say.

"Fifth inning? That tall girl? I pitched it right on the spot, right where Blakely framed it. I even slapped my butt to throw the girls' timing off. And dang if the bitch didn't still homer off of me!"

You laugh, though you probably weren't supposed to. Regardless, our pitcher has already crossed the street, onto other things. By the time your laughter stops, she's onto something else. As if on cue, she switches out the glove for her cellphone.

Anyway, the carpool shift doesn't wait. You meet. You greet. You dodge Pathfinders and Broncos, something you almost didn't do one morning four years ago. Kids look fresh on this day – they won't before long as their lack of sleep and excess of texting will keep them awake long after designated curfews.

Throw in studying and they'll be running on fumes somewhere between Labor Day and Thanksgiving – if not before.

The sun is fully awake now – it's here, a presence, and though the scene is more normal now, the memory lingers like a college morning hangover. Unlike the hangover, however, this one leaves a smile.

Hold the phone, here comes one of your favorites.

"Reese, what are you doing here already? You're actually going to be on time for class!"

She adjusts her way-too-big backpack, shifts it across those athletic shoulders, shoves her phone into her pocket. "Yeah, I'm turning over a new brick this year."

"Isn't it 'turning over a new leaf?'"

"Whatev."

You want to continue the conversation though this one is a verb – an active one at that – and you borrow her energy from time to time and on odd days. Unfortunately, though, and like the softball pitcher, she is gone.

Verbs, after all, have no use for periods or commas. Onward. Movement. Let's go.

The shift ends. Lots of pleasantries. "How many days before Thanksgiving break?" "Are you playing hoops this year?" "Who does football play Friday and where?"

You cross the street yourself, no road raged drivers endangering you at the moment. You cross over the Lower School parking lot, past the speakers that are blasting out "Islands in the Stream," an 80s tune if there ever was one.

The building – your building – looms in front of you, you can almost see the doorway turn into a beckoning finger. It's mid-semester, agenda-filled days, and things to do are now in full swing. Verbs still must be seen to, protected like bumpers on bumper pool tables, prodded, encouraged, preached to, sought after, ignored when needed. You've read somewhere there's a balance to all this, but you think balance is an underrated word nowadays, gone with the 8-track tape players and gridiron stars who do not dance in the end zone after touchdowns.

Everything's overkill. Sports. Academics. Even clubs. People don't rest enough, sit enough, chill enough. Life forces you to grow up too fast, and, like it or not, you're a part of it – maybe a part of the problem.

Regardless, at least God showed up.

And he was just in time. After all, class is about to start again, and he got here just before A block at 8:15.

Don't be late.

HEARTFELT CLASSROOM GESTURES

There's a math class going on – eight or so students in the audience – and the kids are taking up only the middle three rows. Something about kids – they stick together like ticks, often whether they know each other that well or not.

Anyway, in the center of the middle row is a boy named Billy, and if you look 'socially awkward' up in the dictionary, not only will his picture be there, but he'd have been forced to autograph it. He mostly keeps to himself and is often the kid way over there while the rest of the students are over here if you catch my drift.

On this day, Billy is troubled, something is hurting him and hurting him badly. In hindsight, he perhaps should've asked to go see the nurse or the counselor, but he never, I mean never, wants attention, so instead - as a couple tears run out of his eyes - he simply puts his head down on his desk.

Now, to his left sits Tammy and she doesn't particularly know Billy – they'd pass in the halls but, truth be known, if years later something was to happen to him, she'd have to look him up in the yearbook to remember who he was.

Regardless, she sees him out of the corner of her eye, sees the tears, and her heart moves. Don't get me wrong, kids can be mean, but it is this author's belief that God stays busy hour after hour not counting sins and judging, but instead finding cracks in the armors in adolescent heads – tries to introduce them to their souls while they're learning algebra, flirting, and such.

In moving on, Tammy – now connected with the Heavens – quietly turns her desk towards Billy. She does it quickly and she doesn't know why – she just feels it. When this happens, the other few in the class notice, find it more interesting than reducing fractions, realize something is going on.

So it comes to pass that they, too, turn their desks towards Billy, now leaving him encircled – quarantined if you will - as if now protected from anymore evils, hurts, or pains. The teacher, to his credit, does nothing to stop this, but continues his lecture.

The math lesson continues, the students turn in their seats and try to listen, but then Billy lifts his head briefly, sees what's going on. It embarrasses him, quite frankly, but he gives his troubled head a little nod, the only 'thank you' his broken heart can muster.

Finally, the class ends. The students rearrange their desks, Billy's head's still down. But as each kid leaves the class, they don't do it until all put their hands on his young back. Think a football team, exiting the locker room, touching something for good luck.

This leaves the teacher and Billy, and the teacher patiently waits – another class to get to but this is more important - and the student eventually lifts his heavy head, grabs his book bag, and prepares to make his own departure.

The two are now at the exit. The teacher stops, lets Billy go first.

Billy's head is still down, but he does so …but not before putting his hand on his teacher's back before walking out the door.

THAT FRIDAY, FROLICKY, FREEDOM, FEELING

A good thought hits while awaking this morning: It's Friday.

This means so many things, but the first is gazing at your dresser, realizing you don't have to put on the 'big boy' pants but instead can go with the blue jeans. Back in the day, when a commercial defined America as 'baseball, apple pie, and Chevrolet', they forgot to include blue jeans.

They've always been here. Hopefully, always will be.

Anyway, there's a Friday vibe in the hallways – in the fall it's escalated by the night's forthcoming football game, cheerleaders in carpool making drivers honk their horns. Still, even without the gridiron classics, there's still that freedom feeling, knowing a bell will ring and the adolescent jail will end – at least for a couple days – and they can be accountable for less.

So much less, though it's not just the students that feel this way.

"Yes, it's the jeans, but for me it's also these boots," a teacher said as she points downward. "They are like my slippers and one of the first thoughts out of my head is 'Thank you, God!'"

It's the hard that makes it great – Tom Hanks said that in a movie once – and it's that freedom thing, said freedom that's not realized until you don't have it anymore.

In moving on then, all of the above adds more layers to your smile, lightens your step, and even hard days are manageable because there's a point in just a few hours where you can plop down in the chair, mix yourself a Sprite if you want, and at least temporarily suspend giving a damn.

A problem with 'humanness" is that many don't take that time, saying they're too busy. Busy is overrated, you think, as you grab rolls for three teachers after carpool, prepare to "bounce" as the sub man just accurately worded it.

Still…the word bounce – another good word. After all, on Monday's you're practically told you're to slink into the carpets as you walk, bury yourselves in meetings and agendas and plans and committees while the printers print, the ink runs dry, and the brain over-spins and over-analyses and over-assigns.

Regardless, it helps to enjoy journeys when a break is forthcoming, which leads you to this short story:

You once had the chore of subbing for seniors the last day before Spring Break. Think Friday plus a week off plus beach plans, plus alarm clocks set for days later, full tank of gas, road trips, all that and then some.

Think what you will of that but, if God does make notes of our sins, you smile knowing he'll let you slide with a week's worth of them for that and that alone.

No, you're not cut out to be a veteran, probably possess the physical bravery of a daffodil in a hurricane. But you've been on the battle lines between school and Spring Break freedom. And perhaps the most dangerous thing you've done is position yourself at the door when the bell finally rang.

Back to present moment: It shouldn't be that bad on this day – it's a late fall day and the kids probably don't have their beach tans worked out yet. Football season is rolling along though the winter sports teams are starting to schedule workouts.

Anyway, and in closing, the bell just rang. It's late morning if it matters and kids are scattering everywhere and perhaps a bit quicker than normal.

As for you, you're in the middle of it. Wearing your jeans. No weekend agenda which is great when you're older.

So, as you watch them go in and out of class, up and down the stairs, in and out of buildings, you just have to smile.

Happy weekend.

THE TEAMMATE

Once upon a time there was this girl – maybe a freshman, maybe a sophomore – but it doesn't really matter.

She was on the basketball team at her school, and though she couldn't shoot the 3 off the dribble, run the floor with the gazelles, or box out with the big ones, she could live and lead with her soul.

And while the superstars shined, headlines glared in bold font, she silently offered towels among the high noise when the name players left the court, stood, and cheered, always showed up. Once, when a coach was away on baby leave, she sat next to the Head Honcho and kept the shot charts.

It didn't matter that she wasn't really sure what shot charts were, she simply learned and she kept them. After all, a good teammate is like water – it fills the necessary gaps and in a refreshing way.

Anyway, a quick digression:

One night in Macon at a Division III basketball game, the sound system wasn't working and there the fans all were, hands over their hearts, waiting on the National Anthem. The coach tapped his center on the shoulder, pointed to mid court.

The center trotted to center stage, among the 127 or so in attendance, and, without a microphone, belted out the National Anthem like it's never been belted before. Think not 9/11 but the day after, when the anthem was sung and all went crazy in a good unity kind of way.

One minute she's blessing her country, the next she's running the floor, giving up the ball on the 3-on-2 fast break.

Yeah, that, but let's get back to The Teammate.

On this particular night, the scoreboard was racking up numbers in a very one-sided way – don't remember which side it was working for but even that doesn't matter. So, with a smile on her face, the coach, bless her heart, took the clipboard away from The Teammate and sent her off to the floor.

The crowd, what little there was of it, knew something was afoot, so they put down their cellphones and gazed back to the court. As for The Teammate, she was a bit perplexed.

After all, she enjoyed pointing the spotlight, not standing before it.

Anyway, as the Heavens would have it, the Teammate now has the ball around the top of the key. The other four, though taught to flash out of the paint and move without the ball, instead pointed skyway, to a hole 10 feet up.

A duck out of water and maybe not even enjoying all this, the Teammate let it fly and, when the moon's tilted right, I can still see that ball, almost as in slow motion.

The ball swishes the net, the place erupts, the Teammate's mouth flies open. Sure, a teammate is water, but often it's forced to be like a good cook as well, in that you have to throw everything you have in there, sometimes more than the recipe requires, maybe some you're not sure you have. Still, if you mean well, it comes out okay.

So, you cook. You clap. You lead. You follow.

In moving on, the buzzer sounded, though many in the stands hung around because that's the thing about magic - it's like the ending of a great movie in that you want to stay close to it, and the farther you move away from it then the news and the oil changes and the haircuts take over.

God slows us down in different ways, on this night He did it with a 5-3-inch girl, who liked to sit at the end of the bench and cheer on her teammates.

In closing, we've seen our share of buzzer baskets, celebrations, agonies, all that. Growing up a male – though perhaps my 8th grade football coach wouldn't agree – it was usually about bigger, stronger, faster.

Still, water flows. And with that said, the behind the scenes hero now lifted into glory, perhaps didn't know what to do or think about what just transpired. Regardless, her soul as usual knew exactly how to respond.

So, with that said, she walked to the end of the bench, cleaned up the mess, picked up the towels, then joined her teammates in the locker room.

THE ART OF DATING – OR LACK THEREOF

Hopefully I've changed, but I didn't have a lot to offer a woman back in the high school dating life back in the 70s. As a tennis player, my serve wouldn't have gotten a speeding ticket, my PSAT score made my parents officially "worried," and I dared not flex my muscles the way the football players did.

I tried it once and the response, from a coach, was "Compound W will get rid of that wart."

But I knew the definition of a rational number, how to spell Yastrzemski regarding the great Red Sox outfielder, and I proved once that there really was a pop group called The Double Bubble Trading Card Company of Philadelphia. And as my ace in the hole, I had pictures of Paul, George, John, and Ringo.

Still, I would save that one when begging for a kiss at the door, right after the tense music left my head when we looked into each other's eyes on the stairwell.

Kind of a 'Wonder Years' moment if you will - think Kevin Arnold and Winnie Cooper.

The problem was my "arsenal" took up about seven minutes – max – in conversation time. The rest of the night you prayed the movie was good and that your $20 bill would cover her sandwich and the cost of two movie tickets.

Think about that. Twenty dollars? Nowadays you could park half your car for that, register online for where to find the other half.

It was then I decided, somehow or another, I'd make my living as an entertainer of some sort. God, after all, had to be laughing his halo off at my attempts at being a stud in a football/cheerleader type of world, pitied me because the bully did kick sand in my face, and felt even worse when I got bigger than him and he did it again anyway.

Jesus wept. And I remained very nervous.

Still, those were the days when I didn't know you should ask them out to their face, as that made it harder for them to say no. This resulted in dialing six of their seven phone numbers, then slamming the cradle down in fear. A busy signal gave you a reprieve, but it only prolonged things – like when the music starts in a scary movie, and you know something is going to jump out of that closet.

Regardless, I learned resiliency in those years, and I'll always be proud of myself once, when asking the girl out and she simply said no. "Would you care to elaborate on that?" was my follow up.

She didn't, but she laughed. Looking at it later, it reminds me of the first attempt I made at writing something funny in the Horseshoe Bend tennis shop and I heard people laughing.

I was hooked. Still am.

Later in life it was about the glamour girl and the body and the tan. That never worked for me, because I prefer shorts, a hat, and a T-shirt – the natural look. So, my friends dated visions while I poured through the mystery section in bookstores, wrote in my diary and hid it in my closet – where it sits to this very day.

What have I learned? Sometimes you have to let things unfold as they will – like that college basketball player told me when I forced that shot during tryouts. "Let the game come to you, bud," he said.

I'll never forget that.

Present day, no one cares about that singing group,

our kids don't know who Carl Yastrzemski is, and stating formulas only reminds them they have two quizzes and a paper due this week. Two of the Beatles have exited stage left.

But in closing, this past May – our boys' track team won state – there was a video of the 4 X 400 where our quartet brought it home. The video was complete with interviews of our four. I showed my girlfriend the video – my ego dreaming of rings on my finger, applause at assembly, names in newspapers.

She watched, listened closely to the interview of our four kids. And then she said this: "I hope my daughters meet nice boys like that." And that was all...

And I was hooked.

Still am.

Peace and love...

A PICTURE FOR WHITTY

Before every Friday football game, our players go down to the Lower School and read to the second graders. This past season was no exception – the 7-year-olds gathered around while their gridiron role models sent them into new, creative worlds with captivating stories.

Senior Leighton Dickson, a personable soul if there ever was one, waved goodbye to the youth after the final storybook was closed one Friday, and, in what he considered later as an off-hand remark, yelled out, "You guys come to the game tonight!"

One second grader – Whitty Kloberdanz – took Leighton's comment to heart.

"He went home and told his mom he had to come to the game, Leighton needs me!" Leighton recalled later.

Fast forward and get the picture: The game is over, it ended in a tough-to-swallow Final Four loss to the four-time defending state champs. Leighton, feeling the emotional impact of having just played in his last football game, feeling the impact of the undefeated season getting spoiled, was one of many in tears.

There was weeping and gnashing of teeth. There were hugs. There were high-fives, well-wishes, congrats, and every condolence and congratulations possible thrown into one. Parents joined in while coaches spoke, put things in perspective, gave their final love to each and every one of the 16 seniors and the younger cast of characters to boot. It was a crowd scene.

In moving on with the story, out of nowhere, came one Whitty Kloberdanz.

"I felt something tugging at my shoulder; it was Whitty," Leighton remembered. "Somewhere along the line I'd told him that Cheez-It's was my favorite snack."

Now, picture this: Getting down to our field after the game is no easy feat. After all, half are going upstairs, back to the exit, while the other half are going down, out to the field. Ankles have sprained, balance has been lost, shoving inadvertently happens on the that walk up, or down, those bleachers.

This did not faze young Whitty, who simply tugged at his mom's sleeve, got some money, and fought his way to the concession stand before it closed – also not an easy task. Concessions stands, after all, are sometimes known to shut down BEFORE the final horn – all employees involved are generally in a hurry to get off into their weekends.

And also consider this: While most after-game football huddles feature just the players and the coaches, ours is different. All are welcome – on any given Friday you will find aunts, uncles, nephews, sisters, grandparents – if you look closely, you're liable to find a couple of animals and trapeze artists in there.

It's our-school-family thing. All you have to bring are your love and compassion. And in this case, a snack for a hero.

In moving on, young Whitty, money in hand, conquered all obstacles, dodged all large people, got his Cheez-it's, worked his way past EVERYONE and EVERYTHING. And he found Leighton.

"He handed them to me, and I hugged him," Leighton said. Even better, there were parents around, cameras in hand, a photo-op of all photo-ops you might say.

Leighton choked back the tears and smiled big. Whitty, already on the moon, shrank down to his normal three-foot-two-inch size. The two smiled, arm in arm.

In closing this feel-good tale, it was reported Whitty

went home and told his mom it was the greatest night of his life. And his persistence wasn't yet finished - he found a copy of that picture – the one taken that night.

It's in his room, for the record.

And it is framed…

SUPERHERO DAY

It's Superhero Day at school – as part of our Homecoming Week. As I faced my closet this morning, I enjoyed not thinking like a normal human, so instead of the usual suspects, I immediately eliminated all of the Batman, Superman, Wonder Woman stereotypes.

Still, what to do?

My mind went back to the 60s, standing in my P.F. Flyers after being motivated by Jonny Quest cartoons. Complete with the ring that I think came with the shoes, I lifted it to the sky, knowing full well I could now leap over tall buildings. Blessed with an imagination, I think I actually gave it a try, though I'm quite sure I jumped straight into Hunter Reid's mailbox.

Still, what to do?

There's Willie in the cafeteria, who walks most everywhere he goes, punches two clocks, and lifts the spirit of everyone he passes by. And trust me, his Size 9s do pass by quickly. There are teachers, God bless them, and I think of my mother every time I sit at a desk and how unworthy I am to be sitting there.

There's dad. Some of my coaches. Pistol Pete Maravich. Robin Williams. The truck drivers, health care people, and the delivery people that let us all know who the real heroes were during COVID.

Then, it hit me.

With ear buds in the living room, an unwashed hoodie staring at me in the closet, jeans with holes in them, socks that should've been thrown out sometime during the Clinton administration, and a hat that I can wear sideways with the best of them, I grinned while I donned my gear.

After all, I want to dress as a kid. Sure, I hear you, all that "Kids these days!" as I at least try to be a point guard and see both sides, though fail I often do.

Still, they've been dropped before us during interesting times, COVID and political unrest being only some of it. They have 20-plus people to please each day, and a brain that's in over-use mode while trying to do it. Think running a marathon, but with undeveloped legs, that's as good as I can say it.

Regardless, I felt more normal dressed as a kid – as wearing a cape would make me laugh on the spot, a suit and tie, even more comical. I don't know of those heroes, nor do I have any curiosity about them, but I can only close with this and I'm not sure whether I heard it somewhere or I'm now writing it from the successes and failures of my own phone booth – the library.

It is simple, as it is only this:

They say everyone gets at least 15 minutes of fame. Being a kid in this day and time is the least should get them an entire day. And probably a lot more.

Happy Superheroes Day, no cape required…

HER LAST RACE

You see the last of your junior varsity runners crossing the finish line, you record their times, close your notebook, begin to walk off.

But hold it. Wait. There's this one – the blonde over there. There are tears rolling freely out of her eyes, so much so she bends over, grabs her knees. At first, you're confused – then slowly, you get it.

It was her last race. That's it.

This girl, for the record, wasn't born with the "running gene," but like many before her, she just loved being on a team, training with the girls. Putting on the bib number on odd Saturdays. Griping about waking up early on those Saturday's because that's a big part of what running cross country is. Pasta dinners. Looking at course maps. All that, and then some.

She came to every practice, never complained, did all the workouts, helped pick up the mess teenagers always leave around the place. There's a beauty in that, and in junior varsity sports in general. You, as a coach, were once asked what you thought of JV sports and, usually one to wince when reading your own words, remain proud of these:

"JV sports is just like boxing out in basketball. You don't get the stat or the love, but you're the reason why it happened in the first place. JV works just as hard, and they push the varsity where they can stay on varsity."

In moving on, you don't approach this girl as sometimes – in fact lots of times – you let the kids work through things. In this case, think Bambi, but with the momma deer already gone. Instead, you watch as she leans up, walks to the tent, sits down, begins taking off her spikes.

As for you, you prepare to do one of the toughest things there is to do as a coach, and that is give that speech to ones, like her, who have just completed their last high school race.

After all, during the season it is ALWAYS about the next game, next year, gelling for postseason, making it happen. For some seniors, good or bad, it's all already happened.

There is pain and emotion in postgame huddles for many an upperclassman. My favorites are when the coach just shuts up and gives his player a hug – what's to say anyway? Ironic that I say this, but sometimes words aren't necessary, but simply the art of being there.

As for now, you watch while she gathers her stuff, accepts, and gives hugs, briefly cries on her bestie's shoulder. Part of your heart shatters in seeing this, as an adult you always want to swoop in and, well, just make things right again.

And this pain isn't just for the coaches and the kids, either. Moms have cried when washing the dirty uniform one last time, got weepy again when they packed it up, handed it in – this time knowing they'd never get it back.

Dr. Seuss told us not to cry because it's over but to smile because it happened. Easier said than done, because sometimes that final buzzer sounds so – well – final as you walk off that court. You chose to stand out there awhile, even while the other team celebrated around you. It's like when you open the doors of Groesbeck Hall for the seniors come May, many who will never walk back in.

Still, this is a good pain, because it means you – and she – cared, gave a rip, re-lived races when she was supposed to be asleep, pulled teammates aside in the hallways talking of this mutual bond, this team thing with all its sayings about there being no "I" in the word and all that. It's like you always say about running camp – you can tell that you did it right by the size of the lump in your throat when you drive away.

For now, you watch while she walks back to the bus, one last time. She stops once, looks back at the course, at that pain, and that spot right **there** where it began to hurt, and that 100 meter stretch of long, flat grass where she grinded it for all she was worth.

She wipes another tear out of her eye and you could almost swear you can read her mind during all this.

Still, if you had to tell her anything, if words were necessary and a lot of the time they aren't, you'd tell her to rest for a while, be sad if she wants, then get up, get ready, and go get involved in something else she'll love so much she'll cry about that later as well.

It's called passion for life - and that's a good thing...

As she gets on the bus, she catches your eye, and behind all those tears, you could almost swear you see her smile.

ROAD TRIP

Though this road trip was a cross country one, all coaches and students should be able to relate. Collecting equipment, gathering kids, plugging in directions, not to mention the competition itself is something that's part of what we all do. Still, each trip evokes memories – just wanted to share this one.

So onward. Get on the bus. Competition – and more importantly – memories await.

The End

You guess the road trip must've gone pretty well, considering some of your runners just climbed up on a giant, wooden mushroom with both of their trophies and they're posing for a picture. Perhaps that sounds like a scene from One Flew Over the Cuckoo's Nest, but it's real.

There they all, still energetic – a couple of the young ones are even wanting to run for milkshakes at Chick Fil-A even though you've just given the athletic credit card a hernia buying them all pizzas – everything from gluten free to extra meat.

You just watch all this – you can't remember even noticing the giant mushroom but then again, how can you not notice something like that? Still, even if you do, you'd never think to actually climb the thing, particularly since your teenage days happened somewhere before the Reagan Administration.

Still, in your world, it's 8:30 p.m. on a school night. Do you know where your bed is?

Unfortunately, it's 94 minutes away according to

whatever these new devices are called – Waze or Google or is there a difference?

The kids eventually climb down from that beanstalk thing and board the bus, a few of them fighting over who gets to hold the trophies, one riding the other piggyback, two of them appear to be flirting with each other and you laugh, remembering your awkward days of trying to do the same.

Six hours earlier…

It's 2:15 p.m., do you know where your cross country team is? Twenty-two are on the list, twenty-one are present. There's always one, you know? "He's changing, he'll be here in five," one of them said. "He just texted, he's in the bathroom," chimes in another.

Collecting kids, though vital, is ironically the last thing on the check list when preparing for these trips. "Do we pack the tent?" "Who's got the tarp?" "Did the team mom drop the snacks off?" "Where are we going anyway?" "Do we have the athletic credit card, or should I max out mine for the food?"

Finally, the last kid gets on – the door almost literally hits him in the butt on his way in, opposite of the saying if you think about it. Ear buds are put in, books opened, naps beginning – the drool-infested stage later to set in. The pecking order is maintained – seniors with the prime seats in the back, juniors almost there but not quite, sophomores and freshmen scattered across the middle, coaches in front.

Our skipper re-reads the GPS, heads for I-75 south. You wish him not God-speed, but instead that he's taking us on a bus that doesn't break down off the Johnstonville Road exit – ala three years ago. Still, your stomach moves, recalling that day – memories of driving parents' trucks to the meet, practically stuffing 80-pound runners into consoles and glove boxes, frantically making phone calls. All that comes up, the memories fight for air space, one boxes out the other.

Still, that wasn't funny then. Not really sure it is now. Still, as a writer you do love a good story – you're just not sure you want to be a part of all of them.

Snaps shots from the race itself...

The starting line – boys' race. Our star senior is talking to the 14 about to run. The stud is not running today – he's fresh off a win at Wingfoot just five days earlier. Clad in shorts and a black coat, he's pumping them up while the rest of the team are arm-in-arm, facing him.

Think a football huddle, but with too many men on the field.

"Nobody here's worked harder than we have. Nobody. Let's leave here letting everybody know who we are."

You pull out your phone and take a picture of this. At those 14, so hanging on every word from that teammate who runs faster than not only them – but of most everyone – in most every state. They are smiling, the freshmen are eating this up – this guy addressing them. They belong. They've earned it.

You, the coach, stay out of the way. This is good stuff – what you do it for even. Kids bond, win or lose, the young find their place while the older ones learn how to give back. It happens, often before your very eyes or, in this case, at the starting line of the FDP Peake Invitational in Macon.

The star is finished. The player's hug.

One more snapshot: The girls' also at the starting line, do their striders. They're now 100 meters or so out, in a huddle of their own. What are they saying? Who knows? Maybe how mean their coaches are for keeping them out late on a school night. Maybe about weekend plans, perhaps something about the race itself. Maybe about that nerd in physics class.

Still, good picture – you later get the photographer to send it to you. Six girls – one team – massive energy and adrenaline. Standing together on some grassy field in Macon.

Home

There's no traffic on I-75. Due to the storm and the state of Florida evacuating up north, you wonder how that is. Still, when God winks, you accept and say thank you. You get up and count heads once again as, you've learned. If you leave with 22, it's a good idea to return with the same number.

Some emails, after all, you don't want to get. Phone calls, too, for that matter.

And later, the final chapter: Waiting in the parking lot for all the kids to get picked up. Two are still flirting – the guys doing pretty good by the way. You would take notes, but you've already lost that battle – badly if you're keeping score at home.

Eventually, they're all gone except for one. There's always one, as I said earlier. She's a senior, has a car, can legally drive – said car is right here in the parking lot right here in Atlanta.

Problem is she left her keys in Macon.

You laugh. Join her at her car while she waits for a ride. You joke about college essays, the third mile, how she hopes her mother would be here soon. Another coach joins the conversation.

And finally, and for the record, the coach pulls out his cellphone to take a picture – just one more and why not? After all, kids don't write in diaries anymore, they have cellphones that have erased all the words. A bit sad in your opinion, yet there it is.

Still, arm in arm – you pose with the kid, and you smile. Her ride eventually comes and, with a wave, off she goes.

As for you, your bed awaits. Another day to get ready for, another week to put in the books.

You laugh as you drive away, with memories of kids climbing on giant mushrooms, holding onto each other at finish lines, posing for pictures at the restaurant. Your runner's speech while he's garnering attention that perhaps rivaled a Gandhi or a Martin Luther talk.

All that, all good – and with that, off you go.

After all, tomorrow is another day…

NOT SO FAST WITH THIS GROWING UP THING

I'm glad I grew up when I did.

When sports did NOT overlap, when it was okay to apply for only two or three colleges, when I did NOT take mock ACT and SAT tests and I only took the real SAT only once. It was never demanded I be perfect, but instead to just do my best.

When we acted up, the teacher or head dog could paddle us and this wasn't a lawsuit, nor did my parents intervene. Gasp, once a coach grabbed me by the collar and "helped" me into my seat. I deserved it, so I pouted for a day and then went about my business of enjoying weekend sleepovers, impromptu thump football games between classes, or gossiping about the new hot girl in chemistry class.

At night, I had bedtime, and I did this often forgotten thing called getting some sleep.

Poll a high school kid now, I dare you. If I had to put my non-math skills to work, I'd say they average four hours sleep per night tops. No, they hear but don't listen if you tell them they need sleep, but when I throw in that they'd flirt better with a better rested body and mind, NOW I have an audience.

Now they have AP tests and tutors and private coaches, not one said coach that will tell a kid simply to go rest. No, there's no money in that. Instead, it's strive and strive and strive instead of enjoying being young, energetic, and alive.

It's not the 70s anymore. There was even a meme out a few years ago about being perfect, about how if everyone was even 99% effective there would be five figures worth of undelivered New York Times out there.

Something like that. And throw in the terrors of comparing on social media and we have ourselves a perfect storm.

One of my many roles at school is that of a coach. The advice I give most often is very simple. "Enjoy this! Slow down! Take it all in!"

Just this past May I was part of the problem – hurrying from class to graduation practice to state track to write my story and call my girlfriend and collect some scores and post the information out for a world that has to have yet something else to read.

My part is to slow down myself. Because once upon a time I played smear football in the fall, shot hoops in the winter, then traded in my sneakers for a tennis racket in the spring.

We played outdoors until mom called us for dinner, then we played some more. The only pressures I ever felt upon me were those I put on myself, and unfortunately that was many, but I never got that from mom, nor from my dad.

It's now the land of too much, too quick, overkill, big, bigger, biggest, good, better, best. A world hurrying them to grow up, where they can get a job only to wish they were young again.

Once in another part of time, I witnessed a meeting where high school FRESHMEN were told about the job market.

To me, their jobs are to be youthful and goofy and energetic, enjoying each other in the hallways after forgetting to cram for a test. If they play on a team, do your best, and may the coaches not coach to the less than one percent that go pro, but instead as much if not more from the end of your bench.

I envy these kids and yet feel sorry for them at the exact same time. If I were in their shoes, I simply couldn't do it, and I think I was known as a decent student/athlete once upon a time.

If done the way it is, now, however, I would've sought a counselor when there wasn't one, or been too scared of what other's would think even if I did.

Lastly, there's a kid sitting in the library now where I'm subbing. He's asleep.

Guess what? I'm not going to wake him...

EVERYTHING I KNOW, I LEARNED THROUGH CARPOOL

"Carpool is never going to change; therefore, I'm going to have to."

I said that to myself back in 2010, back when our beloved Pathfinders and Broncos were backed up beyond Mt. Vernon, maybe even to Hammond, possibly to Utah. Horns. Angry voices. Glares. Frustrations.

I'd go home those days so mad I wouldn't even run from my pet roach – instead I'd chase that ugly bastard across the floor and shoo him into the closet. (Don't worry, he always comes back.)

My anger angered me. I am flawed, wacked, often mentally ill, disturbed, and self-absorbed, but I am nice. My mother taught me that. I'm not supposed to admit this, but I may disappoint the God above me, but I don't want to end this life upsetting my sweet mother.

If you knew her, you'd understand.

Anyway, one day during the winter, a man actually rolled down his window in freezing temperatures, put down his coffee to do it, and yelled something mean. Now, my smart aleck voice that I perfected in my college days, had the ideal punishment for him.

May his window get stuck in the down position, may his tie get frozen around his neck. Not too tight, but tight enough, if you get my drift.

Still, the new me thought: You don't know this guy. Maybe he's getting up the nerve to tell his wife he's coming out of the closet. Maybe she's already told him that she has. Maybe the exterminator killed the dog instead of the termites.

Who knows?

One day, our line was backed up to Phoenix because a lady was texting. My instincts told me that the least I could do was smash her window, confiscate her belongings, and call our head of security. I mean, he's nice, but he does carry a gun...

Then I thought: What do I know? Maybe she just found out her cat reproduced. Now they have eight more. I know I'd hold up carpool line if I found out I had eight more cats to feed. Wouldn't you?

As a writer I try to summarize things, and I do feel – actually I know – that the world needs more point guards, people that see the whole floor. Instead, we're cursed with shooting guards that only see their own goals.

Still, one day....it happened.

It was winter, times 12. God hit me with three degrees, 20 miles per hour winds, precipitation. Mother Nature laughed at my five layers, and the wet in my shoes had festered into my socks. I was sneezing. If you're a runner, you're familiar with the phrase "snot rocket."

I'd just set the world record.

But then, a car pulled up, a window rolled down, and an arm reached out. It was one of my runners, someone I'd watch win, lose, draw, cry tears of joy and tears of triumph. Our van broke down once and we couldn't determine which one of us was more clueless in getting it fixed.

Regardless, and to put it blunt, I'm glad it was sleeting; I didn't want people to know it was actually tears that were dropping out of my eyes when I walked inside. Anyway, I kept that box for a month, probably didn't eat the donut for a week. Maybe not at all.

In moving on, it's not about losing who you are, but

it's not about losing your peace either. I didn't cause the Pathfinder to almost run over our sweet nurse, but it's in my life so I'm responsible for dealing with it.

So maybe the sentence extends..." life isn't going to change, so maybe I have to."

Ah, there's the sentence that gives me goosebumps, actually made me put down my wine and write it down.

In closing, I was in Dunkin Donuts the other day. Who walked in but that student, that runner, that non-mechanic. Coaching, teaching, memories, are savoring bonds. Think the end of movies, when the music picks up and the dad is tossing the baseball with his kid. Something like that – I think it was "Field of Dreams." Not sure.

Anyway, all I know is this: I walked over. Gave her a hug. Bought her a cup of coffee. She didn't want a donut. I thought it might be rude in offering her mine – that one from last February.

This made me laugh. As does my education through carpool. And life its own self.

DATING AS A YOUTH, "DATING" NOWADAYS

I interviewed a recent high school graduate today – am always curious about the late adolescent mind and how they process things; the obstacles they face with social media, pressures to grow up too fast, all that.

The subject of dating came up. And I wish to share how TOTALLY different things are nowadays.

Correct me if I'm wrong because I often am, but I remember it this way: You asked the girl out to her face, because it was easier for her to say no if you called her on the phone. You picked her up at her house, being nervous about meeting her parents – said father often was cleaning his gun while you stood next to his prized possession.

Not only did he ask your agenda and tell you when she needed to be home but perhaps, for an exclamation point, he would "accidentally" point said gun at you. If you remember correctly, you may have peed a little, but let's move on.

You opened the door for your date, paid for her dinner and whatever you two did. In the end, you walked her to the door and hoped she'd kiss you. During the date – the seat in the car was one, long flat one – where she sat was often a key point.

On Monday, one of the questions often was, "Where did she sit?" Obviously, if she sat close, your heart raced, the future looked bright. If she sat on the other side, however, you were screwed. (Actually, you weren't, but you see my point.)

I explained this to this 18-year-old before me, and then she told me this and, of course, I'm paraphrasing because I can no longer write fast enough to keep up with the teenage mind, mouth, or changing tracks on the fly.

Dates are usually formed on Group Chats. You meet them out. Prom, in fact, the kids got in buses and were taken to their destination. Guys do not like to be seen on dates, that has them known as "simps." I had never heard that word until today – in our day it meant you were "whipped" and I won't repeat the other word that went with that.

You no longer ask a girl to dance, everyone jumps around in a large puppy huddle. Meeting the parents, walking them to the door, and the nerves of asking them out in the first place no longer exist. This saddens me though I always forget the part where no one asked.

I told the girl I was talking to that perhaps it was more romantic back then, and in fact, at our own school we used to give prizes for the most creative ways of asking a girl out. Once upon a time, a college buddy put his woman on a parasail, wrote "Will you marry me" in the sand, and met her upon landing with champagne and a ring.

I find all this as rites of passages, part of life, the girl saying yes or the girl saying no the equivalent of winning or losing the big game. Quite simply, it's a part of growing up and becoming who you are.

It's a different world – a different dynamic. And though I envy the youth in their technological opportunities, I'm a bit saddened by the lack of face-to-face encounters of being chiseled into becoming a man or a woman.

Once upon a time, I dialed the first six numbers of my object of affection's phone number, then celebrated because her line was busy. I was scared. But going ahead and doing it anyway was a big step for a nerd like me, a challenge that had to be overcome.

My interview subject felt sad that it isn't that way anymore – told me she wanted to be courted that way. I wish this for her as well – she provided life at our school and will continue to do so at her college.

Anyway, the interview ended and, as always, I'm the one who became the most educated. Still, in my Madison bred habits and infused with at least some of the good sense of my mother, I opened the door for her as she left, walked her to the parking lot to make sure she got there okay.

After all, Group Chat be damned – a lot of life is learned face-to-face, and a big part of who you become is learned from a short distance, and perhaps never electronically.

Soul to soul...

CHRISTMAS BREAK THOUGHTS

In all due respect to Jesus, inspirational speakers, self-help seminars, and meditating until you fall asleep on your mat, it was working at a high school that lifted me from the ashes. Don't get me wrong, it's not like my view now is from above the penthouses and the skyline, it's just that – when I got to the school years ago – it was somewhat well below that.

Very well below I should say.

It was 2007, and I had driven up from Florida – survived the boredom of nine hours of pavement hell, the only sound the droning of my tires over the pavement that never changed. Though they teach and preach location, location, location, the beach, hotel tubs, palm trees, and tiki bars in the Sunshine State hadn't served me well.

On my final night – while the gin and tonic lifted up my arrogant side – I'd even declared the God of All Those Sayings wrong when I stated that it's actually location, chemistry, and timing that's so important – each just as vital depending on the situation.

I was, after all, well versed in cracking on sayings and I learned that from my dad. A memory: He HATED the saying "absence makes the heart grow fonder." I can still see him, throwing down the paper after reading those words and almost yelling, "They didn't finish the saying! It's actually 'absence makes the heart grow fonder...of someone else!"

I was just a child then, though now I'm old enough – experienced enough – to believe him.

Moving on, I pretty much lived in a penthouse down there until my wife suggested I re-locate, and I'd driven up knowing two things: First, I'll get over her. Second, I doubt I'll ever get over my dog.

People always laugh when I say that, though I'm only telling the truth. Then again, maybe that's what makes it so funny – the simple truths and all that.

In hopefully making these words a rag to riches book of essays, let me briefly go into the mind set of this at the beginning. When I moved back home in the Atlanta area, I owned one couch, three shirts, and five figures of debt. When I inserted my ATM card, handcuffs came out. I was financing counseling.

Not sure if you've ever been through the hell of depression, but my first day in the hallways, it was almost as if the world – in this case the students – were all moving in fast motion. The world appears that way when you're troubled.

After all, everyone seems to have somewhere to go. A life. Except you. I still recall that day in fall semester of 2007 - after the bells had already sounded and the kids had littered, loitered, flirted, filed things in their lockers, and had already entered their next class, there I was just standing out there – dazed, a "what the hell just happened" kind of feeling, or a boxer on the ropes who'd just taken a few shots.

Unlike the demands we often make of the world, getting back to normal isn't a quick fix, a gulping down of Effexor's until the brain rewired. Instead, it was one class at a time, one kid at a time, one game, one story, one season.

I pray you recover as I did, as the world looked rather dismal through eyes with no vision, lost hope, ex-flames, and broken dreams. Still, before I go on – and I know this may be a bit strange – but I have to throw in a tribute to my old dog here. Get the picture:

I'm in Florida, sitting on the stairwell, head in hands.

There's not much furniture in the condo anymore, the ex has relocated, complete with removing both our names off the phone bill, Florida Power, all that.

Anyway, my dog – a 26-pound Basenji with as many hours of energy in a day as his weight, walked up the stairs – I can still hear the bell attached to his neck ringing with each paw print. He dropped his hind legs, sat right beside me, and looked up as if to say, "What's next master? Where are we going?"

To this very day, years later, I can still cry a tear of a bit of happiness at that scene – at that unconditional love, that trust, that belief in his master. And when the moon is right, I can still see the confused look on that little guy's face when he would lift up his hind legs and then pee all over his front ones.

Priceless. Pets can be that way.

Anyway, let's get to school. The kids are here, stories, truths, and lies are flying all over the place, the halls and walls overwhelmed by syllables and sounds. The writer in me wants to hear them all, but …. There's work to be done.

All in good time.

After all, a school year is a marathon, not a sprint…

THE GIFT

In an art class at the corner of our campus, a student/artist sits in the window, the sun angling in lighting up her young face. She notices nothing in the world except the palette laid out upon her crossed knees, her hands, and eyes are a part of her work.

There are other kids in the room – scurrying, shuffling things, a bit loud, conversations everywhere. She, the artist doesn't notice.

That's the thing about art, you know? It lets you turn off your mind and lead with your soul. Maybe the whole world should be that way, but let's move on.

Anyway, the artist doesn't even look up when the teacher moves closer, silently, not wanting to kill the moment. Good coaches and teachers are good that way, too, knowing when to back off and stay away.

Still, the teacher pulls out her cellphone and snaps the picture – that artist, that sun, that palette, that-lost-in-creativity place where ideas and comets and whirlwinds are born. The student looks up, smiles silently, looks back down.

The teacher – before she leaves – approaches just for a second, as she knows and gets what teens go through these days, the saying "you know how kids are these days" be damned. The artist looks up, the teacher leans in and says:

"Don't forget this. This. When life rears its head and kicks you in the butt. Use your gift. In times of trouble and even when not, use your gift."

The student looks up, her head spinning perhaps in a direction of her past. She looks back at the teacher and finally, this: "Yes, I think it may have helped save me."

The teacher smiles, big, then bigger. "Yeah, gifts have a way of doing that." The two tap knuckles, a bond formed much thicker than the paints on the palette.

The teacher then turns and moves away, heads back to the rest of the class...but not before a tear drops out of her eye.

THE TRUTH

The truth is seeing your teammates enjoying each other's company on the bus trip home, and though the scoreboard says you lost, in actuality you did not.

The truth is how cute it was when the student had to go outside to read. When she gets stressed, she has to read aloud, and she didn't want to disturb the rest of the class.

The truth is interior, but we're always taught to rate, value, and judge regarding the exterior.

The truth is being able to yell and scream for help when you need it – it doesn't mean you've given up but instead that you're refusing to.

The truth often lies with the kids at the depth on your bench, because they provide a different view from the ones getting the glory.

The truth isn't how you act among friends, but how well you handle and react when you're not.

The truth happened in art class the other day when a freshman wanted a creative pose so she took off her coat and jumped into the trash can. Not for the grade, mind you, but for the art.

The truth walked by me yesterday. He saw something was wrong with his classmate, so he simply put his hand on his back as he walked by.

The truth was laughing at the freshman when the drink tap exploded onto her face. Her laughter was worth it – because taking yourself too seriously isn't.

The truth once ran a cross country race in her crocs. She'd forgotten her shoes but just wanted to run anyway.

The truth is when one of the coaches told me not to post the score – it was very one-sided and she didn't want to embarrass anybody.

The truth is the adorable, shocked look on the girls' face when told she had to play goalkeeper for a half. It scared her to death, but she did it anyway.

The truth is found in forgiveness, with ironically the toughest one to forgive is yourself.

The truth isn't found on the news – not the real truth anyway.

The truth is a writer wanting to be alive, though without the place he's sitting in perhaps he wouldn't be.

The truth hopefully won't remain hidden…the trick is to be okay with all the good things about you that comes out when it surfaces.

The truth is the fear felt before speaking in chapel, because if you're not scared perhaps you don't deserve to be up there in the first place, or maybe you're not saying anything worth listening to.

In light and in truth…

A REALLY COOL THING THAT HAPPENED

It seems the 5th graders ran into the classroom all excited one day, so much so that the teacher couldn't understand what they were saying. Twenty-one little voices, all at once. Think a movie with no script – just excited people yelling, but in a happy way.

The clamor was there's this senior here – who is a many-time state champion already signed with a big college - this senior who is breaking finish line tapes in times that have people shaking their heads. Even has my email lighting up.

Anyway, the senior was either heading into or out of one of our buildings while the 5th graders were walking in. He was approached by one of those little angels – she held a piece of paper and a pen.

She wanted his autograph.

Now before moving on, this senior is a person who shakes every coaches' hand after every practice. Or gives us knuckles or high-fives or whatever the going thing is

He signed the girls' paper. And the next boys. And so it went down the line.

Christmas came early for those little kids – and it did so because of a kid who's not under the saying of "You know how kids are these days!" – but instead a role model. On the course. And off it.

The 5th grade teacher is a good friend of mine. She shared this with me. With so many bad things out there, I just had to share this.

Because there are good people out there. Good things.

And because of a good deed, there are and were a lot of 10-year-olds last week that were elevated to the moon because of it.

What's that worth? Having your kid be that happy instead of mad or stressed?

Signing off, going to get an autograph of my own...

CONVERSATIONS IN ART CLASS

Get the picture: It's 8:15 – first period. It's an art class, so some are scurrying around looking for their projects and their paintings and their potteries, others are in "stare at computer and cellphone" positions. The last semester seniors are fashionably late and being cool about it. Eventually, they all plop down, like it or not.

I read them the laws: No cellphones. Clean up when you're finished. Then, amongst groans, I present the lesson plan.

And then…I listen…

"The swim coach tried to put me in a relay. NO WAY I'm doing a relay – that way I'd tick three other girls off!"

"What'd you tell the coach?"

"That I'd be more than happy to bring cookies and take pictures."

"Did she go for that?"

"No way! She tried to teach me the flip turn. Didn't work. Still, I like swimming, it lets me zone out."

"But don't you get bored?"

"No, I just drift off inside my head."

"I don't know, I like running – at least there you have different things to look at as opposed to staring at a black line at the bottom of a pool."

Another girl chimes in: "Oh my God! Running! I told my mom yesterday I was going running. She was, like, why?" And I said, 'because I'm fit now!" She was confused and asked me, like, how'd you get fit?" I said, "I don't know, but I feel fit."

"So, how was your run?"

"I made it about the distance of one or two laps around the track. Then walked home. I hate running."

Five minutes later:

"Do you guys know that sophomore girl who was in the library a while ago?"

"Who are you talking about?"

"You know…that thin girl. She's…kind of emo in a crystal sort of way."

"What the hell is 'emo in a crystal sort of way?'"

"You know – kind of hippie-ish, a rock necklace around her neck, and she has those eyelash thingies going on – sort of black and thick. Sort of like a hippie but not wearing black. Sort of goth perhaps."

And later: "I'm getting cramps. For the rest of the week, I'm going to use that as my 'Get Out of Jail Free' card. I mean, I don't use it much."

"Yeah, don't blame you."

"I mean, if I go through this for days out of every month, then I should be able to do this, right?"

"Heck yes, you should SO use that. I'd use it all the time."

Another voice: "Think of this: that's a fourth of your life, and you sleep for a third of it. That's, like, a LOT of your life! You should – and we should – be able to use every card we can get our hands on."

"Word!"

Later: "Look, Coach Dunn, I'm triple jointed!"

"What? How exactly?"

"Watch!" I watch while she stretches one of her arms, full out, and touches the wall. Instead of her arm bending the natural way, however, the top of hers goes the other way and sort of twists – again against the grain. "Wow," is all I can manage.

"No, wait, I'm not finished." She turns her arm down,

the other way, and once again, the rest of her arm rebels, defies gravity and natural law. It looks…. painful.

"I bet you wouldn't have a problem getting out of those straight jacket thingies the cops put you in." I say, proud I remembered a Mel Gibson scene from one of those "Lethal Weapon" movies, but not so much about using the word "thingies." Perhaps I've been here too long. But still.

"Oh, I could SO get out of one of those jackets!"

And finally, one more:

"Nora, why is your hair still wet?"

"I know, don't nag me. I was walking out of the house and my mom told me not to go outside with my hair wet or I'd catch cold. I told her that she also tells me not to be late for school, so pick one!"

"That's pretty funny."

"She didn't see it that way."

Eventually, the bell rings. I stand at the door while they file out, some as if shot out of a cannon, others more deliberate, one specifically to avoid an unfinished Spanish assignment. Regardless, as I watch them go, I have to laugh because – even though I'm not sure they learned much – I know that I learned a lot.

Always do.

See you at lunch…

MAKING THE PRESENTATION
(Adolescent Flashback)

Later in life, you would learn that the second biggest fear – behind death – is that of public speaking.

Fear – you knew what the word meant already, mind you. It was batting off Donnie Curtis in Little League baseball – he at the age of 12, already standing 6-for-3 and probably shaving. It was carrying the ball up the middle as a 110-pound halfback against defenders perhaps bigger than Donnie, with full beards and college scouts in the stands.

It was opening a pack of baseball cards and finding no bubble gum inside. Calling the cheerleader for a date, only to chicken out before all the numbers were dialed. Finding out there would be no more Columbo episodes.

But, as usual, I digress.

To be clear, there are many layers of fear when you prepare for this presentation thingie. First, you have to come up with the idea that will keep your friends awake, while at the same time please the teacher. Then, you must wake up the night before in a cold sweat wondering if you should scrap the whole thing and start over. There are more: what to wear, how to keep your knees from shaking, if the length is too short or too long.

But perhaps most of all – maybe even past the fear of dying itself – is that first moment when you stand before your peers. Just you. Naked. Alone. Your normally loud classmates silent. Looking at you. Waiting on you.

I knew then that teaching would simply have to be the hardest profession in the world as we know it. Think about it: doing this EVERY DAY – class after class after class! And to think, a lot of the time – maybe even most of the time – their pupils don't want to be there.

You'd learn later that there's a high suicide rate among dentists. After all, nobody wants to go see them. May teachers NEVER enter into that statistical category but instead know they are the most underrated heroes and human beings who will ever grace this planet.

More underrated even, than the beloved Hank Aaron of Atlanta Braves fan. Or Tracy Grant. (She got cut from the cheerleading squad in college. Another story. Please don't ask.)

In moving on, I wrote a poem. It was about going to prom with one date and coming home with another. And how you really shouldn't try that because NO ONE will be very happy – not only including your date, or dates, but both sets of parents, next of kin, and all who will attend both family reunions.

My thinking was that it was sort of funny, without considering that one of the victims was in the audience, her mother already sternly telling her to "stay away from that boy." And her boyfriend was sitting next to her – he to this day doesn't find that amusing, though I always thought there was a statute of limitations on that sort of thing.

Who knew the formula of "too soon" as opposed to "that's awesome."

I didn't. And I was about to prove it.

It came to pass that the day arrived when I had to face my regular irregulars, partners in crime, mischievous mates, but had to do it in serious fashion. Could I pull off the impossible – make them laugh, consider me cool, maybe even include me on their shenanigans over the weekend?

Removing most of the pizza stains from my shirt, taking the cardboard out of the collar of my new shirt –

because forgetting to do that is terribly embarrassing – up to the front I went. There were 18 or so of them out there, though it seemed like about 450.

In looking back, maybe the teacher counted off because I never looked up at the audience. Maybe it was saying "um" about 38 times. Perhaps it was the sweat pouring profusely onto my new shirt, messing up my Vitalis-ed up hair. Maybe it was the thought of going from two dates down to zero.

Still, I found it odd how much they laughed, before, during, and after my talk. And I didn't die, not yet anyway, and I passed. Maybe out of pity but I passed. My classmates, though perhaps not knowing what the hell I was talking about, just smiled at me even after I sat. There were snickers going around the room. Even the ex-date and her boyfriend seemed quite pleased with me.

Wow, this was great, I thought, maybe I'm a comedian. After all, I was funny when I wasn't even trying to be funny.

Later, in the hallways however, it all became clear.

It wasn't my presentation after all, nor the delivery, the subject matter, the theme or the length. It wasn't my dress or my cardboard-less new shirt or my scrubbed away pizza stains. It wasn't even the pitch of my voice or my posture while delivering it.

It was simply the fact that my fly was open…

I wonder how much she counted off for that.

SO, YOU WANT TO BE A COLLEGE CHEERLEADER?

When Margaux Ventulett was a little girl, she remembers watching college football with her family, and being mesmerized by the cheerleaders and all they did. The seed was planted, a seed that would slowly but surely germinate as the days wore on.

"I liked the idea of cheering in college even back then," Margaux said. "Still, I didn't know if I could ever get there, or if I'd ever have the skills I'd need to do it. Moving on to this past school year, I remember after the first practice how much I'd been looking forward to it, and how – after next year – I simply couldn't and can't imagine my cheer days coming to an end."

Margaux, who went on to participate in competitive cheer through Middle School along with cheering for both football and basketball all three years of her high school days, went home after the above practice and mentioned her collegiate cheer plan to her dad.

"He was supportive, told me to go for it; he also told me to talk to (HIES coach Amanda) Peckham and get some info from her."

Since then, our acrobatic junior has been following the bouncing ball, which led her to websites and now clinics, into her gym to work on her skills. One weekend, for example, she participated in a clinic at UGA; one break found her in Knoxville investigating the possibilities of continuing on at Tennessee.

"Going into Georgia last weekend, I was nervous, excited, fired up, scared – all of the above," she added. "After all, I'm not really good about walking into a big group all by myself – I'm used to having a group with me."

Fortunately for Margaux, the UGA beginning was a positive one, as all there were very encouraging, telling her she had what it takes, prodded her to keep on keeping on.

Still, it's the moving on part that many don't understand – the competitiveness, the having to gain the extra edge, the almost cutthroat possibilities of getting dismissed on the spot, and the skills – not only physically but mentally - that must be honed and sharpened to reach the coveted rainbow.

"The college tryout process for cheerleading is like no other sport," Coach Peckham said. "Every school varies a little with requirement, but most have multiple rounds of the tryout with cuts at the end of each round. Every year, cheerleaders have to try out for their school's cheer program. No one is guaranteed a spot year to year meaning all new and past cheerleaders are trying out together."

Coach Peckham is no stranger to schooling HIES student/athletes into the college world as, in her 15-plus years on our campus, seven have moved on to the college ranks.

"Rising college freshman and transfer students will fly in from all over the US for tryouts and for some, they may only last through the first round of cuts," Coach Peckham added. "Tryouts are also open, meaning any one can sit in on the tryout. I've been in the stands of Stegeman Coliseum at UGA watching one of our girls make it through first cuts and then coached her through what skill to perform for round 2. I've been in the gym while another one made it to the interview process after two rounds of cuts at Georgia Tech. It's nerve wracking for everyone involved. Coaches just help keep their cheerleader's mind at ease and walk them through what skill they have that will make them stand out to the judges in that next round."

Perhaps many don't know this but cheerleading at the high school level isn't exactly a piece of cake in itself, either.

"It's actually upsetting to me that some people put down something I enjoy so much," Margaux said. "Many say it's not a sport and so forth, but we work out in the weight room, practice before and after school, dance, stunt, choreograph, learn 40 to 50 cheers, and then some."

Margaux recalled one Winterfest a year ago where her team – after months of before and after school sessions – performed the final routine three times in the same day. "And that isn't taking into account the cheering during the game," Margaux added.

One of Margaux's teammates this past year, Mary Bowden Wilkins, also had another aspect to add.

"On top of everything, you still have to have 'the look,'" Wilkins said. "I was looking online at a college cheer site, and they always say you have to be 'Game Ready,' which includes hair and make-up. You have to look good, yet at the same time be ready to get tossed into the air all day."

Margaux was in complete agreement.

"The look is important especially for flyers," she said. "They must look the best because that's who most of the people are looking at. Also, you have to make it look effortless while looking good doing it."

Margaux, a flyer herself, added yet another element to it.

"You also have to trust your bases," she said. "This used to affect cheering for me – once I started trusting the people down there more, that totally changed and switched my mind set."

And now here is Margaux, slight in stature but huge in spirit. After UT this weekend, she's considering going to Florida State. If not, it's back to the gym and high school tryouts and meetings and getting ready for next year.

"It's all highly competitive," she said. "It's all about being better than you were last year. And, if you take time off, there's somebody out there getting ahead of you."

Looking ahead to Margaux's senior year, it's college essays and classes and pleasing parents and teachers and coaches, all this while socializing and trying to enjoy being an upperclassman. Still, there's a dream lurking out there, one that keeps her going, one she hopes will keep her pom-poms in the air.

If she's cut at the collegiate level, "she'll be just a number being announced," added Coach Peckham. "If your number is called, your journey is over." If not, there's a possibility of only being an appearance cheerleader with limited games; others may make the next level that performs stunts at home and some away games.

Regardless, there's a gleam in little Margaux's eyes when she talks about this, a passive competitiveness if you will. She's a girl about to be thrown into a cutthroat type environment. She must be physically fit, mentally tough, able to handle the nerves and the pressure.

Ah, and don't forget, she has to have the right hair and look during all this.

The positive, end result, however, is a great thing, as Coach Peckham remembers the carrot of putting on that uniform in front of a crowd, knowing that it was all worth it. As for Margaux, perhaps it's that passion from her coach that gives her the extra lift – hopefully the lift needed when the time comes.

And God Bless and love our Margaux, as she continues to move into and out of the hallways to the athletic fields, to clinics and to two-a-days, to weight rooms and to the sidelines, while the whole time staying ready to give the college cheerleading world all the great that she's got.

LEAN, LEARN, LIFT, AND LOVE

Whether you're a voice in the hall, a doctor in an office, a construction worker handling machinery, or regardless, sometimes things get tough. I wrote this in February, during a turbulent time. The socks weren't matching up, the tires needed balancing and, way more importantly, I couldn't bring myself to cancel my Valentine dinner reservations since I no longer had a Valentine. Anyway, I hope this helps . . .

Dunkin Donuts. Early, way too early. My friend and colleague Willie walks in, plops down, closes his eyes. There's rain in the forecast, another "Seattle" day ahead. We discuss the groundhog briefly but realize neither of us give a damn what he saw or said or did.

Why's it up to a groundhog, anyway? I prefer birds, but nobody asked.

The drive to school is six minutes. Five redlights. Sometimes a deer, almost always cyclists. He fires off a gripe, I rally with one back. He laughs. Hard. The seat of my Honda actually moves. By the time we pull in, we're laughing, lucky, okay.

Yesterday a teacher handed me a book, signed it over to me. It's called "The Boy, the Mole, the Fox, and the Horse." You can read it in ten minutes but it will help in 20 lifetimes. I guess my posture and mood was heavy, the book helped.

I payed it forward in the hallways, reciting one of our Lady Bear basketball players stats from the night before as she walked past. "How do you know all that?" she asked.

Because when you're around care, you care right back, that's how. Besides, there once was a day when all my days centered around whether a round, orange ball went into a hole in the sky, or where an optic yellow tennis ball did or didn't land.

Speaking of, I had a call from a high school friend and classmate last night. Random. Out of the blue. Just checking in. Making sure all is well.

I hung up the phone and I smiled.

Later - moving through the hallways, I can actually feel all the agendas, the non-linear-ness of the moods. It's a curse of being a writer, you "feel" too much sometime but I wouldn't trade it for anything. Besides, my job is to run it through the mixer, try to make sense of it, translate it into love and peace and hope and joy.

I succeed sometime and I feel closer to God. I fail sometime and it adds pain to more pain. Still, it's what I signed up for and my dad – who's birthday is today by the way – would never let me quit.

Moving on, a student asks if I can help her with her math. I laugh. Loud. From the belly. This from a boy who once closed Rome, Georgia celebrating from a C in Math 101. Still, she wanted help. And again, there was laughter.

The librarian tells us to quiet down.

It's worth it.

Simple moments, simple things, connections. Bonds.

Sometimes the trick – even during rough patches – is to realize how lucky you are. My body aches in more ways than one, but I'll walk among 571 or so today – 571 stories, moods, agendas, randomness, awkwardness, athleticism, and goofiness.

And, on the work front, when winter sports mix with spring, I'm often not sure whether I'm scratching my watch or winding my butt.

But Willie made me laugh. A teacher gave me a book

that made me cry. There's a rhythm to all this and some-times it feels chaotic, crazy, crucial, chronic.

With that said, and in between classes when the library is empty and the boss lady has left the building, I walk to the window, stare out at the quad, the kids, the chaos. I actually scream because sometimes I'm weird that way.

And my scream was a prayer – and it was only three words.

Keep it coming.

A DAY IN THE LIFE OF A DRAMA TEACHER

It's an hour before "show time, go time", do you know where your cast of characters are?

There's a couple of them in the corner, another one files in, but where's Joel? And did his mother forget the flowers? And was Suzie at school today, you never saw her. And can anybody do her part if she doesn't show?

You are backstage while your mind is all over suburban Atlanta and then some, you're gazing at the props, wondering if they look right, will fit right, will blend with the scene and whether the people and the audience will notice. The costumes, uniforms, fake beards, glasses, wigs, and moustaches are strewn in front of you, waiting on those energetic youngsters – those verbs you call them – to come in and disguise themselves.

You hate the hour or so before the curtains open. Then again, you love it just as much. Did we go over that last scene enough? Or too much? You wonder, yet you can wonder all you want but there's one sentence in life that simply cannot be refuted: There's no telling what's going to happen when you're dealing with young adolescents.

Absolutely none.

A text comes in at the same time your phone rings, at the same time two of your cast walk in the door, at the same time one of them already has a question. Attention deficit disorder? Don't leave home without it – or what do you do for a living if you don't have it?

Anyway, his moustache won't stay on, one of the set pieces is bending, cracking, the loosely put together table getting closer by the second to becoming a rectangle – or worse. According to the text, the co-star's voice is fading and do you have a fill-in if necessary? One calls with good news – the cupcakes will be ready when the curtains close again.

Still, closing curtains – though only two hours away, might as well be an eternity. No time to worry now, however, you must put out fires, calm young nerves, contain uncontainable energy, channel it, focus it, propel it onto stage in front of an audience you hope will laugh. And cry.

And if all else fails, at least hope they will understand…

In moving on, you're a solution oriented soul if nothing else. The moustache is glued on, emoji's are sent regarding texts, your fill-in is average at best but she can read the lines if necessary. As for one, he seems nervous but at least he's here. You peak through the curtain – people are filling in, chatting, relaxing. They have the easy part, just sit in a comfortable chair and if all else fails – if you and your cast fail, that is – they can go to sleep, get lost in their cellphones, send emails.

With 20 minutes to go, the last kid wanders in – there's always one allergic to being on time, at least one – and when she files in, they are all in front of you, disguised, made up, wigged up, psyched up, amped up.

And you without your Advil.

You relax them best you can, tell them to take deep breaths, to forget that momma is watching, and let them know there's not a teacher out there grading them, there will be no marks on their permanent record, whatever that is.

With five minutes to go, some sit alone, praying to every God that ever existed that they won't forget their lines, their cues, their exits. They hope their wigs are making it a better hair day than they already had, that their loved ones won't notice if they flub their lines.

As for you, it's a hopeless, helpless sort of time. After all, there's nothing left to be done. You've practiced, laughed, cried, yelled, emailed notes and fixes about the props, set, and costumes, begged and pleaded for people to attend – PLEASE attend – or perhaps maybe not.

Let go and trust. Breathe in. Breathe out.

And just like that – after months of rehearsal, a curtain opens, the lights are on, and you – more than a little nervous yourself – must go out and address what you hope is a crowd.

You remember as you stride onto the stage that there are two huge fears in life. One of them is death. The second…public speaking.

Still, you smile. The parents – most of them anyway – seem sweet and understanding and anxious to see their loved one. You, not much of a speaker, understand the three rules of it at least – be brief, be brilliant, be gone.

You don't know about the brilliant part, but you nail the other two, make your exit, and wonder what kind of sense of humor God has to lay your future in the hands of 12 year old kids – none of which has yet seen a zit, a date, or keys to their own car.

Your knees shake as you take your seat backstage.

Moving on: Gene nailed it, Ellie was adorably awful but the adorable part got her through it. Billy seemed nervous but being he's young enough where the cute factor made the audience pull for him that much more.

The tech crew running lights were flawless, the music way too loud at first – causing many in the audience to jump, perhaps wet their legs a little, but that was quickly fixed.

The show, for you, lasted about six days – though in actuality 54 minutes as you've timed it. With a sigh, you peer out at an audience that appears rapt, some using their phones as cameras, many smiling at their dear loved one.

You breathe out at least 74 pounds. Try to make yourself relax.

But not for long, as the last scene is key. Romeo must kiss Juliet, though Romeo is 12 and he's scared crap-less of Juliet in real life – in fact she might even have the cooties. Not sure, but do they still have cootie shots at that age?

To heck with on camera smoothness, you think, just kiss the little girl, and make it look almost believable. Please!

Anyway, you're proud of him, it's not an Oscar winning hug and kiss, but he sort of enfolds her as if she doesn't have but some of the latest COVID virus. He looks into her eyes and it almost appears he likes her.

As for her, her eyes are closed, lips puckered out, and you laugh to yourself knowing she's more than afraid of receiving a kiss she does not want, and perhaps she's wondering why God put her in this position.

Her first kiss? In a play? In front of her mom? Really?

It's awkwardly, inept and clumsy and goofy, and almost horrible, but it's so dang cute when they pull it off. As for you, you clap and you smile and you laugh while your innards move more than the world's most awkward rollercoaster.

Regardless, as your cast comes off the stage, those cute little bastards dressed in togas and beards and attire that doesn't quite fit, those girls in those…whatever they're called those things that will never fit just right.

Still, they hug each other, high five, give each other knucks, all of the above. They did it! We did it! Encore! Take a bow! Curtain call! Shine the lights on us!

You watch from afar, you're funny that way – maybe there's a writer in you that has to take it all down before being able to make sense of it all. Then again, how exactly do you do that – take 11 and 12 year old's and throw them onto a stage before their minds and nerves are even close to developed, their guts still in the embryo stage.

Maybe your job is to make calm out of chaos, order out of riots. Maybe it simply can't be done.

Who knows? But still, maybe that's where the humor of it all is, you know? Mixing what can't be mixed, doing what can't be done and then charging ahead full bore anyway? Maybe that's life its life its own self, and the adventure is in seeing the final result.

You put down your notes, breathe out Texas and half of Missouri, the applause still ringing inside your tired skull. You look over at your cast – you stay where you are not wanting to kill their moment – and you just stand and admire, perhaps in a gloating mom sort of way.

And before you approach them, and later after you leave them, you just can't help but smile.

And you're still doing this as the stage lights dim and fades to black.

Exit stage left.

The End.

FERRIS BUEHLER HAD IT RIGHT

The library. Early. The sun's still asleep and I hope it announces its presence with authority. A track meet is ahead – 28 degrees – a day of hypothermia before later a sun burn, back to hypothermia again.

Ferris Buehler had it right, life really does move pretty fast. Putting it on paper is my way of slowing down, trying to make sense of all this.

After the last finish line has been crossed, the final baton passed, and the officials frantically punch computer buttons to hand results out to coaches, I hope to end the day belly up in Chattanooga, enjoying my Sprite.

I sat in that establishment so long last time I ended up checking IDs. Not kidding, and it was kinda fun. You meet all kinds of people when you take the time.

My personal rule I just established while writing this: While out, cellphone REMAINS in pocket! We're living in a world where, since everyone is tuned into their phones, they're tuning out to so much more.

Like last night: A wanna be boxer. A sports couple that knows every stat – including the beloved Pistol Pete's. The work ethic of the owner, who didn't have time to talk because he had to run French fries to Table #8. A waitress who took the time to tell me about the time she ran track – or tried to.

I promise I don't write these things to tick people off, but it's my way of remembering. And if I ever went back to college – I've already been twice – I'd write more down simply because how priceless, and dangerous, and interesting, and adventurous – college life is.

One day I drove nine hours from Florida unannounced for interviews no one at Holy Innocents' had scheduled me for, and I told them I wasn't applying anywhere else because I wanted to work HERE. All of a sudden, I'm looking my 20th year in the eye. Who knows, I might even get a transistor radio or something at an assembly, be noticed for getting so old.

Something I read, that to me should be remembered: Everybody needs three things – something to do, something to love, and something to look forward to.

Perhaps we've had days of going 0-for-3 in that department, maybe getting one or two right. I think the middle answer leads to the other two though I'll skip the part where nobody asked.

Enough from me, I must go. Besides track, there's regular season baseball today; region final hoops' tonight. There's a story in every pitch, every dribble, every coach-player conversation.

For now, though, I simply stand at the window, look out at an empty, dark quad. It's a scary movie – the silence of a campus, the absence of noise, no feet and locker sounds, no voices.

That's okay though, because it's the silence between the notes that makes the song, the empty space in the rooms that make them rooms to begin with.

I forever long for the balance in both – the A and the Z and all in between.

Thank you. Just thank you.

A DAY IN THE LIFE OF SUBBING

You're at the front of the room, the lesson plan already read and currently being ignored. There are six in here, all seniors, all suffering from various forms of senioritis. Like the common cold and tennis elbow, there's no known cure. Still, listening is free . . .

"Describe me in one word, but the word can't be 'jerk.'"
"I wasn't going to call you a jerk!"
"Thanks."
"And can the word be hyphenated?"
The girl looks to the rest of the class – her eyes quickly scanning the group, turning them into judges – hoping for a ruling. Two give thumbs up, one doesn't seem to give a rat's behind, the other's wheels are spinning but no words are coming out.
"Okay, we'll come back to that. How's this – if I were to write an essay about hanging out in senior commons, what would I write?"
"There's a skinless corpse in there!"
"There's a what?"
"Not really, it's just every time I say that I get the same reaction you just gave."
"Nice."
"Seriously, though, some sleep so long and hard you do have to check their pulse."
"We go in there to zone out."
"And eat."
"Some go in that room, close the door and study. Well, sometimes. Sometimes they just go in there and close the door."
"I'd describe you as inquisitive." (Somehow the game switched, not sure how. Just when you thought you had

high school lingo and the minds cornered, they dribble out of danger, confound you once again. You laugh. Out loud.)

"What's so funny?"

"You all are."

Wheels spin at this statement, but nothing comes out. There's a pause. And then.

"Abbie, have you studied your kinesiology?"

"No, I have swimming and then I'm baby-sitting."

There wasn't a comment for that, but in the corner "The Ugandan Tyrant" came up, whatever that is.

"It's an immature quality to want to conquer the world."

"Wouldn't it suck to travel all the time? You would, like, always have jet lag. I mean, it's 3:20 a.m. in Beijing right now – 8:20 in Germany."

"Fidel Castro was 6-foot-3, or 6-foot-4 – he actually played basketball and ran track. There's a video of him playing basketball. Hold on." We wait for his hands to do the walking and Google to do the talking, and finally, "Look, there he is, playing hoops."

"Wow, he came off the screen pretty well. That's text-book – right off the shoulder. Gets the rock and shoots it. Wait, there's more!"

"Why is Abigail laughing?"

No one's sure, but she really IS laughing. Her face is shaking a bit, glasses are moving up and down a bit. It's the kind of laugh that's contagious. Soon, giggling breaks out, no one's sure why.

Except maybe Abigail.

"I watched a two-part documentary on Tiger Woods."

"Nice. My dad says if he hadn't cheated on his wife, he'd still be the best golfer."

"I like him as a golfer – though he probably shouldn't have gotten married."

"Didn't she, like, club him with a 2-iron or something?"

"I thought it was a wedge. Probably hurt either way."

"I interviewed Jack Nicholas one time."

"REALLY!"

"Yeah, scared me to death. He was my dad's hero."

"What'd you talk about?"

"Wheaties."

"Wheaties?"

"Yeah, he got his picture on the box."

"Nice! You know you've made it when you're on a Wheaties's box."

"Word."

"Also, if you're a crossword clue. How cool would that be?"

"What would be the question?"

"Or the answer?"

More spinning wheels. A bit of quiet. And then...

"I'm not an M.I.T. guy – I don't like college algebra."

"How do you know, you're not in college yet."

"Yeah, but if it blows in high school, why am I going to look into it when I get to college?"

"Hard to argue that. I wouldn't know – I got wait listed at Georgia."

"They won't let you know until April, right?"

"Right. Isn't that kinda rude – like your date telling you the day before she can't go to prom?"

"Who was that that threw up last year at prom?"

"Oh yeah, what was her name...."

"I'm going to get a face tattoo of John Steinbeck and live in the woods. Outside of school, I love being alone. I want to stay in a cabin someday, though I'd have to take a gun to shoot bears."

"You should get one of those Fire Watch jobs, have you ever heard of those?"

Eventually, your hands get tired, your head exhausted from its spin from Uganda to prom to golf courses to Fidel Castro. Abigail's not laughing anymore, Google is at rest. Senior feet are propped on the desks, books long forgotten, computers closed. There's 23 minutes left in class, but the brain, even the random parts, appear to be winding down.

The last minutes move slowly, often seemingly backwards. Eventually, the bell does ring. Bags, computers, sports equipment are all gathered up. They file out slowly – they're seniors after all – they walk cool and calm and collected.

You listen as they go, the words are a blur – though you hear something about the beach, another giving directions… to somewhere.

Still, another day, another class is marked off the box. And as you try to make sense of all this, you laugh as Abigail just did, slowly at first, then in a small uproar. A freshman walks by, sees you, thinks you're crazy.

No problem. You are.

Perhaps that's the fun of all this….

Have a good night…

SPRING BREAK

In Every Town, U.S.A., a huge part of any high school kid's life are these dangerous two words: Spring Break – with both words beginning with capital letters on purpose, regardless of what any style book says.

And before I get into this tale about this former adventure waiting to happen, I must say that if you EVER get the assignment of subbing the last class on the Friday before school lets out for the above break, then bless you. You will not only get a place in Heaven but will have reserved seating – invite all your friends if you need.

While I'm on the subject, and if you're into pain, there's no need to harm yourself with objects or potions. Instead, just stand at the exit door on the above day, face first. I dare you.

I can't think of the above two words without hearing Jackson Browne singing "Running on Empty" back in April years ago, perhaps because that's exactly what my friends and I were doing.

Windows down. Stereo up. Cooler in the back. Feet tapping up front.

There will always be something about freedom that stirs the soul, and I've always said that if you want to watch even adults go a bit crazy, just tell them they don't have to go to work the next few days.

Thankfully, definitions of "crazy" change with the passing years – and if you live long enough, 'crazy' actually becomes throwing an extra blanket on the couch before going to sleep before 9, maybe even two.

In moving on, and perhaps on the other end of the spectrum, I think the harshest punishment we have in the world isn't the death sentence, but instead solitary confinement. No light. No love. Not much room for movement. No Kroger or Walmart anywhere to be found. Without wasting words, eventually you go crazy...

Hence, spring break – where you go crazy in ways of your own choices.

Where I grew up, the thing to do was go to Panama City, Florida and stay at what I think was the Summit, because it was right by the big hot spot – Spinnakers. To give you some logistics, there was a wall between the two places, thus making you walk all the way to the road to get around the wall, before then having to retrack your steps back to the night spot.

One night, with two drinks for wisdom but a much lessened degree of coordination, we decided to simply climb the wall, thus not only saving the steps, but getting us into the place earlier.

After all, there was music. And women. And energy.

The football star goes first and he climbs to the top, then jumps down. Same with friend number two, not athletic but with pogo sticks for legs. Then...it was my turn, and before I could make my approach, I heard a voice behind me.

"Son, what do you think you're doing?"

It was wonderful meeting a Panama City, Florida policeman at this time, don't you think? Him all mean, me all goofy. Him representing the law. Myself flashing off mating genes and "sprite" on my breath, and an eagerness for more of the above.

I just stood there, all 120 pounds of farmer tan, nothing yellow running down my leg. Yet.

"Son, I tell you what I'm going to do," he said. He adjusts his hat and belt as he says this, perhaps adding layers to his words. "I was young once. So...I will give you one chance to get over that wall. However, if you come back over on this side, I'm taking you in. Sound fair?"

Who was I to say no?

He folds his arms, waits. I released some of my Sprite, could feel it oozing down my leg, though for the record, the term "relieving yourself" does NOT apply when a cop is waiting for you to test your high jumping skills, even though you did get statistical credit for pulling one high school basketball rebound in your life.

And that was on a long rebound that Don Gilbert fumbled, but let's move on.

I eyed the wall. The cop eyed me. There was music playing in my head, though I don't really remember if it was ELO or Styx. Didn't matter – neither was any help when there's a high block of cement in front of you.

Counting back from five, I got ready.

"Dunn, what in the hell are you doing?"

It was friends, though it was easy for them to be thoughtful because they'd already been vault-full if you'll pardon the dumb rhyme. "I'm coming...I hope," was all I could say.

Enough. Let's do this. A cop was waiting. And my friends. And women. And adventures.

Taking three quick steps I prepared for the Great Leap of 1978. Problem was, my plant foot slipped as I lifted, therefore I did not "lift" very high. Still, I got high enough to grab the top of the wall with both hands.

And I pulled. Groaned. Screamed. Yelled. Yanked. Every micro-muscle I had got into the action. It was sort of like when Segar had to get over that wall in "An Office and a Gentleman", but I don't think that movie was out yet. Then again, maybe it was...

Anyway, my desire, persistence, and perseverance overrode my lack of muscles. In what seemed like four ELO songs, I made it to the top.

There I was. Doubled over. Gasping for breath. And then I heard it.

The policeman was below me, laughing his butt off. Doubled over. Hat fallen off and on the ground.

Eventually, we locked eyes, two souls that would hopefully never see each other again. And then: "Thanks for the entertainment, son. Have a good night and...please be safe."

I couldn't talk, so I waved, making sure to spread all five fingers where he wouldn't confuse the nice gesture and instead think I was flipping him off. I've always been nice that way. Credit my mom, she taught me.

Anyway, with that, the policeman picked up his hat and went about his business, trying to uphold the law.

I went into Spinnakers, perhaps hoping to break it.

Happy Spring Break...

THE MUSIC MAN

In 1966, I was cast in a play – The Vowels – and I was to be the "A." It was a speaking part – "A as in apple, etc." and the week before I was exciting about how I was going to wow the world, so much so in fact, I was already practicing my post-play speech and how "it was nothing, really!"

Two days before, however, the teacher – in a move that shocks me to this day – pulled me from my role, gave it to Terry Armstead, and made me the silent "Y." So, instead of prancing across in front of the lights and being embraced by Madison, GA, and the rest of America, I said nothing.

Just held the sign, walked across, and my puckered up lips got to the end of the stage about eight steps before I did.

Fast forward 41 years. I've returned from Florida, am now working at a school called Holy Innocents', and it seems our drama department was going to surprise the kids. The play was "The Music Man", the kids would perform but, without them knowing it, the faculty would play the opening train scene.

The kids wouldn't find this out until the day before – when the curtains were drawn and eight of their teachers were on stage.

Being in a bad place in life, I made myself sign up – despite the horrible slight of 1966 where stages made me break out in hives and wet myself to that very day. (It was years before I could even walk in front of a micro-wave, but that's another story.)

We practiced on the sly – Wednesday mornings – and something strange happened while doing so. After all, this could be a psychological experiment – bonding with teachers and Middle Schoolers alike. Getting out of the comfort zone. All that.

Anyway, the day before was priceless. Some of the kids actually broke into tears when they saw us up there. I kinda got goosebumps myself – even as I'm writing this. We did three shows and, I can't forget this: I had a speaking part, which I remember to this very day.

"You really know Harold Hill?"

Okay, the audience wasn't that impressed, either, but there it was. Almost well delivered with the timing of swinging too early at a curve ball. The part I'd envisioned – them stopping the play on the spot to let me sign autographs…. Well, it didn't actually happen that way.

Still, the train rolled on until the final curtain, and those adorable little souls came after us and mopped up any bumpy tracks we may have laid before them.

Still, another memory about that night: It was backstage. Before the play. One of the girls in the cast walked up to me and said, "Do adults get nervous, too?"

I had to edit my answer, as it wouldn't have been appropriate telling her I was about to have an unplanned bowel movement or something gross like that. Instead, I just said yes. She smiled, so brightly.

Connections. That's what it was. Doing something new. Being on equal footing with the kids instead of sitting high on the podium looking down. All for one instead of that generation gap thing. Common goal, common nerves, common anticipation. Common…well… lots of things.

Anyway, one final thought – and it's funny the things you remember.

I'm walking to my car after the final production,

realizing that I am not, nor will I ever be a music man. It's not who I am. Regardless, after going through the entire process – the A, the B-through-Y, and the Z of the whole thing, I just had to admit:

I still sort of felt like singing…

A DAY IN THE LIFE OF
AN UPPER SCHOOL CLASS

"Can we go to the Campus Shop?"

"Who's we? Just you a friend?"

"No, there are 17 of us. Safety is very important."

You laugh. You should say no, but 17 against one, being on the out-numbered side, can cause headaches later during the class. Assuming they return.

One-by-one-by-one and so on, they file out, searching in their oversized bags for their purses or wallets or borrowed-from-their-parents credit cards. "Will you buy me something?" the lone remaining student asks.

"What do you want?"

"Anything with too much sugar. I'm tired."

You call roll as they file out. Check your watch to gauge how long it takes them to raid the store of candy bars, milk duds, bagels, and anything that isn't nailed down or enclosed in a glass cage, though even that's not off limits.

Eventually, they return…

"Okay, please put your cellphones in these hangar/garage thingies up here."

Suddenly, the students' eyes turn into daggers – a touch of hatred mixed with how dare you. Slowly, and you do mean slowly, they get up, rebelliously drop their coveted rectangles that disengage them from the world on an hourly basis, and they drop them in.

Poor souls, they must now face the world bravely, alone, with only their five senses to capture what's left of reality. You actually cry an inner tear at this, even miss the times when girls rejected you outright, but it was face-to-face, ear-to-mouth, soul to soul.

Once upon a time, after all, people communicated before people invented communication devices where we don't communication anymore. What can you say, God has perhaps the greatest sense of humor of all. Figures, right?

"Okay, today we are watching a video and answering the questions on canvas. What you don't finish will be for homework."

You watch the wheel's spinning this very information in these 18 skulls, smiling because x-ray vision only exists for teachers and parents, and it exists where they can literally see the cogs grinding when thoughts are running through heads at 500 words per minutes with gusts up to 1250.

Anyway, you finish reading the "plan", it took approximately 28 seconds. There are now – subtracting the campus shop march that for some reason took 16 minutes – you still have 40 plus minutes of this.

Oh Lord, please take away at least some of their energy.

The students then do what their souls scream against them doing – they sit. Computer tops fly open. Book bags – heavy as you said – destroy the new carpet with the weight as they hit the floor. Earphones go in – not to watch the video – but the Winterfest dance is coming up. Dresses, after all, must be ordered.

And let's not forget the hair. The nails. The after party. The dinner. The date. The, like, is she really going with him?

And then, because even hyperactive minds have to check in on occasion, the harsh reality of being in a classroom sets in. But not for long.

"Can I go to the tech office? The computer ate my

homework." (Wow, times have changed. It used to be the dog!) "Can I go print a paper in the library?" "Can I go to the bathroom?" "Can I go on an adventure?"

"Go on a what?"

"An adventure!" She's gone while you're trying to find a reason to say no.

Five file out here, a bit less than the prior 17. Still the remaining 13 are jealous. After all, they have energy, too.

As for you, you sit, wonder why you didn't go back to grad school, perhaps teach tennis your whole life. Maybe marry rich. Actually, you already did the marry rich thing. She threw you out, made you return to poor.

Memories of sitting alone on a stairwell, with nothing but two shirts, a pair of jeans, no kitchenware, and a dog with diarrhea, come to mind. And, of course, papers to sign.

"Coach Dunn is something wrong?" one asks.

"No, just dreaming of beaches, boats, and birds. Instead of here, getting trampled by kids going to Campus Shop and wondering how much trouble I'm going to get into because of this "go on adventure" thing. Still, thanks for asking."

The clock ticks. The kids – with obviously nothing to do except the lesson plan, start merging, pulling desks together.

After all, high school kids are adhesive – they cling and hug and grab each other – on beach breaks they practically pillage each other for days on end. Once upon a time, you were told to keep them six feet apart. You laugh, as did the kids. Might as well ask water not to be wet.

You remember in the year 2020, in fact, stepping between two attracted by that invisible magnet – magnet existing because God, too, enjoys laughter. The two kids were small, though you didn't have a chance. You came out clawed, bloody, injured, in pain.

Even the nurse was impressed by the depth of your wounds.

Moving on, five minutes left. The kids are Pavlov's Dogs. They know time even if there is no clock. They begin the arduous task of lifting those bags. Computers are closed. Earphones are off, the adventure girl is nowhere to be found. You remind yourself to read tomorrow's headlines of the AJC, wondering if she's okay and if the key to your office will turn tomorrow as for your job security.

They gather by the door. Gaze at you. They have their cellphones but you remain their captor, you evil bastard. You wonder, just who in the hell died and made you the boss? And why, please tell me why?

"Can we leave Coach Dunn?"

Your mouth starts to move.

They take that as a 'yes.'

And with that, a stampede of 18 heads out, 18 verbs – active verbs – with agendas that will change with every third step, tasks and assignments to be forgotten before they hit the stairs. You start to yell something, but what for?

After all, that part of communication left the building even before cellphones.

Have a great day!

THE RING

Writer's note: In high school sports these days, getting "the ring" after winning state seems as important to them as the victory itself. I was and am fortunate to have been a part of a couple of those. Here is our story:

I wear the ring.

I wear the ring and it reminds me of the further educations of becoming a track coach, reminds me that it takes not only a lot of parts to make a whole, but a lot of good ones. Dedicated ones. Versatile and resilient ones.

There are rings worn for many occasions these days – personally the wedding one didn't work out all that well for me – but there are graduations, rites of passages, and the like that are signified by getting your finger measured, putting on the prize.

But the prize is how you see it, what it does to your gut even if this is written four months to the day after it all went down on that huge campus in Powder Springs. It is more than a piece of bling I see before me, but of those boys, said boys who perhaps aced Resiliency Class back at the pandemic, and they took that to the throwing ring, the pole vaulting area, the high, long, and triple jump pit, the hurdles, the track its own self.

Snapshots come to mind as we pass through this life thing, and I can still see our 100-meter star, already with medals across his tired neck, being asked to rise off the tarp on an 80-plus degree day, asked to get out of his comfort zone, and see if he can help. Just one more time.

Or our leadoff man, who knows the 800 and he knows the 1,600 and he knows cross country, but he has no clue how to come out of the starting blocks. There's laughter in this vision, of our sprint coach taking this young man "out back" and showing him the what's what in the art of the start.

The third man, the unknown, the unheard of – the quiet kid from up East who never factored into a scouting report. He's a polite kid, shy, respectful, and quiet, a kid who ran cross country but blended in.

Now, on the biggest track stage in Georgia, he is asked to step out of the 'player to be named later' picture and not just perform, but instead to stand out.

And our anchor, our heart and soul of most if not all distances, who – when asked later how he felt about getting psyched up for this race – he would simply answer, "To tell the truth, I was kinda tired after the 800 and 1,600. I just wanted to go home and get some rest."

Still, snapshots in my head – and regarding this team – go far beyond the pixels, deeper than what meets the eyes. Because success, no matter how people spin it, takes a village and this village started with a talented team with no pole vaulter and question marks due to injuries.

It began with a coach who had to step back, therefore others who had to step up. It began with background people-now-become leaders, who now to had to stand in the front, be seen, be accounted for.

Once that's done, maybe just maybe it's about getting a percent or so better each day, one throw at a time, one jump at a time, one trip to the river. Maybe cutting a corner off a run really does matter – particularly when you're dealing with micro-seconds, and with tough competition. Maybe two or three-stepping in the hurdles really are big things.

And especially since the season came down to the last event of a three-day meet, where four teams could emerge as the best. As a reporter I always ask swimmers and runners this one question: There are 400 meters left to go in the race and you and your opponent are side by side. Why are you – and we – going to win?

Because sometimes, in order to get it done, mediocre must improve to good, good lifts to great, coaches not only learn the presence but exude it. And it's the whole clan, let's be clear, because not all of the 60-plus on the team had the opportunity or, shall we say, the daunting task of toeing the line with the state of Georgia watching.

Just think, one slip of the baton and we're not even on the podium, whereas a race of perfection has us soon fitted for rings.

Enough about this, enough from me. Still, as I gaze down at my size 9 finger, before this piece of jewelry marks me part of a champion, the feeling as it is placed there does a lot more than cover up a part of my body.

Instead, it's the presence of all emotions – winning, losing, injuries, ice baths, river runs, getting a new pole vault pit, where are the hurdles, what time's the bus leaving – that take turns in line to get to the front for my attention. Think kids waiting to go off the diving board on the first day of summer.

Still, when you mix good with good – good kids, fun coaches, good times, and good times if you catch my drift, and good spirits – however it washes up it ends with a smile on my face as I head to my desk.

Sorry for this. Like many things I write, perhaps this is and was particularly uncalled for. Life, after all, moves forward – new year, new season, new sport, and new cast of characters are now before us. Maybe sometimes things happen, though, that you like to hold on to and, though it can be bad for comparison purposes, sometimes there's a lot to be said for simple self-preservation.

Maybe it's too much pride, sure, that's possible. Maybe I'm just bored. Maybe I must put pen to paper before I can believe it actually happened.

Then again, maybe I'm going to quit apologizing now altogether, whatever the reason.

After all, I wear the ring...

THE SECOND SEMESTER SENIOR MATRIX

Monday morning. Rain. Winterfest Week over. No more trash talking regarding the faculty vs. students basketball game. Costumes are replaced by the normal 'big boy and girl' clothes, the echoes of pep rallies since faded into the carpeted floors, lighted ceilings, long lines in the cafeteria and the Campus Shop.

High-pitched, excited voices are now lowered, volume turned down from a 9 to a 3 if you will. Unlike last week, often you have to lean in in order to hear. It's maybe that in itself that makes the silence so loud.

In moving on, there's a collective quiet – we could call it boredom – permeating these halls. Ironically, as I'm writing this, a student asks to borrow my computer charger.

Perfect. That's what we're all doing – recharging – because it's back to routine.

Bells. Desks. Lectures. Lockers. Lunch. Off to practices. Calculate the days until Friday. Repeat.

I'm subbing for last semester seniors, and I'd say about 33% of them are still here mentally, though their bodies have no choice. Cohesion isn't the order of the day, nor is it synchronicity.

In short, body, mind, and spirit are in at least three different places, probably more.

Senioritis is real – don't ever think otherwise.

It's sort of painful if you think about it. They're pretty much finished but they're not – have been accepted to the world of freedom that is known as college but they're still incarcerated. Their biggest rebellion, in fact, is probably with themselves – more so than the papers, tests, projects, presentations.

Think standing outside on a freezing cold day, seeing the warmth inside, but the problem is the door's locked. Yeah, maybe that's it.

Ironically, I feel their energy even though there's not much in here. Mental fuses fire, too, sure they do. In fact, that's where it all starts anyway.

I weep for them, envy them, want to trade places with them, yet glad I don't get to or have to.

Still, if you could see a matrix of what's in this room it would look like a 15-color checkerboard, neon mixed with plaid mixed with solids. It's called High School, U.S.A. People weep for the teachers and the administrators and I concur.

But I feel for the students as well.

In closing, say what you will, but every year I come to depend on this matrix, rely on it like a crutch after a broken ankle. It's there, it's true, it's real, and it warms me because even though I know my body will grow old, but my mind never will. After all, Winterfest or not, there's still SO much going on.

And oh, you can feel it. You just can't quite see it.

THE LITTLE THINGS

Walking the halls, 1975 or so. My headmaster/coach is walking behind me and, for reasons still unknown, he yelled to me across the distance. "It ain't the big things in life, Dunn, it's the little things."

Funny how some things bounce off, gone faster than heated up molecules, while others lock in, superglue into your soul, doesn't leave thick or thin, or regardless whether or not a relationship sticks till death do you part. In fact, some 45 years later I made a speech with just that title, "The Little Things."

With that said...here are some:

- Random 22-second conversations with the students between classes, talking about nothing, yet at the time perhaps everything.
- Hearing that chili's being served at lunch on a cold, rainy February day.
- Watching the different way student/athletes prepare for a game. Everything from sleep, to headphones, to chattering to that "get the (bleep") away from me" philosophy.
- Our huddle after a football game. At our school, it's not just the team but everybody – students, parents, cheerleaders, grandparents, martians – are allowed in.
- The art of preparing a chapel speech for good kids – the nervousness, tweaking, fear, standing at the podium – hoping you can pry kids from their cellphones where they'll hear your message.
- The feel of a Friday – music up, top down, spirits soaring, and with an agenda consisting of "who cares?"

- Before a cross country race, that Golden Silent Second after "runners to your mark." Then the gun. Then the noise again.
- Speaking of cross country, a November of 2019 day, the moment you realize your team did it. That moment when tears flowed and you hugged someone. Problem is, you weren't really sure who you hugged or if that was one of your parents or not.
- The joy the students give you when you tell them their lesson plan is a study hall.
- Knowing that there's nothing better than a good teacher or coach. Conversely, there's nothing worse than a bad one, either.
- A post-game meal with the coaches, having a Sprite and listening to what they REALLY think about what happened out there.
- Connections. Period.
- Blue jean day. There's just something that makes a school day go better when you're wearing blue jeans.
- Walking past a meeting when you know and appreciate the fact that you don't have to be in it.
- This, from a student last year: "You know, and I'm not sure why, but I always feel a little better and a little calmer when you're in the room with us." One of the best compliments I'll ever receive.
- Having a former student/athlete return to school just to stop in and say hello. Something to note: Wins and losses rarely come up – it's all about the bonds, the adventures, and the memories. This, as it should be.
- That look on the Homecoming King or Queen's face, the split second when they find out they won.

- And the look on a mother's face – any mother – when you say something nice about their kid.
- That second when carpool is over after a freezer cold, blistering wind winter day.
- That day when a student – reason's unknown – stopped, leaned on me for support out of perhaps depression, desperation, or all of the above, then moved on and walked into the classroom. No words, then again, none required.
- When girls' braid each other's hair before games. It's neat seeing people take care of each other – put that on the news will you.
- The constant reminder that "hate is just love without the facts." And here's to the constant pursuit of those very facts.
- I must go, the bell rang and I'm supposed to be somewhere. Not really sure where.

A DAY AMONG POPCORN BRAINS

A random Wednesday. The cafeteria. Winter. Chicken tender day.

If only my cross country kids ran as fast as the students do when they're at the door and find out it's chicken tender day. They'd have to build a new gym to put all our state championship banners, I'd have canned speeches at all the parades, have no more fingers to put my rings.

But God help you if you're in their way. Think, one of those rollers, but with you under it. Once they peeled you up, a bad hair day would be the least of your problems. Weight loss, too, for that matter.

Anyway, someone taps me on the shoulder. I'll call her Sue, particularly since that's her name.

"Joe has a popcorn brain."

My thought: All of you do. We live in a society that produces those. And we're dang good at it. I laugh, recalling a line from the sitcom "Friends', I think Phoebe said it.

"Hello kettle, I'm black!" That one.

For now, I watch Jane's wheels in motion while she's describing Joe – and if my mind could follow the trajectory of hers, it would be like a roller coaster on steroids. And all I'd know is that wherever I got off wouldn't be anywhere close to where I got on. Kids are priceless that way, which reminds me of another sitcom – "Mork and Mindy."

It seems they chose the role of Mindy by whoever could follow Robin Williams when he went off script the best, by who could keep the script or what was left of it, moving forward.

Maybe that's us – we're a bunch of Mindy's – though

there wasn't anywhere in any manual at any time that equipped us for this. It's trial by fire. Sink or swim. Take two thousand syllables of random dribble and fence it into a lesson plan. Contain the uncontainable.

Try it sometime. I dare you.

In moving on, and with her in mid-sentence, she decided to walk off. Something caught those hyperactive eyes, or ears – over-sensed all of her senses perhaps. And to think, I'd almost caught up with where she was going with the conversation.

Close. Oh, so close…

Regardless, I looked around, wanted to find Joe. After all, how and why does he get distinguished above the distinguished, the best at what he does? And, if and when I find him, I'm not sure whether to give him a lecture or be kind of proud of him.

Later: There he is, right there. Joe. A Stephen King novel spread before him, headphones in, a person talking to him at the exact same time. Me, I would faint at the overload, but Joe answers the question, turns the page, bobs his head to God only knows what kind of music.

Joe's friend leaves, I approach. Still, how do you time this? When he's turning the page? During the chorus? When his eyes quit moving.

"Hey coach," he sees me before I'm there. I'm starting to think; students could make excellent Ninjas. And why wouldn't they? After all, they know whether you care or not in about 37 seconds, why could they not sense your approach, whether you mean well or not?

In a way, this is a good thing. After all, caring sets you apart at a lot of places. Here, it's the norm, though it's nice to fit in if you can.

Moving on, I ask Joe about his day. He answers by pulling out the last 10 things he's Googled. I try to draw a linear map in my own non-linear head. He reads them off to me: Population of Ethiopia. The novels of Jack Kerouac. Was Saddam Hussein a good basketball player? The art of making Brunswick stew.

Connect those dots, would you? Once again, I dare you.

He gives me his agenda. Four classes. No advisory (Translation: Major screwing off during that time). Practice. Two projects, one paper, two tests, a sister to either take care of or avoid. Two parents to please. In fact, so many to please. Coaches. Counselors. Advisors. Friends. Teachers.

I counted once – regarding a four-sport athlete with four siblings, with all of the above criteria. I think the final number, counting assistant coaches, was 26. Think: What if she had a bad day, only pleased half of them?

I guess the popcorn only got half buttered, some days maybe not hardly at all.

And besides, at least Jesus faced his flock all at once. As for him, and perhaps all of them, every turn of every corner is an unscheduled test. A paper they may or may not have written. And don't forget homework.

Anyway, you sit outside Senior Commons, hearing things you're perhaps not supposed to hear. Still, you blend well if nothing else, people know you're harmless, a puppy dog with his tail wagging if you will.

Regardless, you have to get the class rolls, get to art, off to carpool, then to practice, collect scores, call your girlfriend, write a story.

You smile. A big one.

After all, the popcorn's still popping, maybe all the way buttered, maybe not.

Keep it popping.

Just keep it popping.

TOO TIRED FOR YET
ANOTHER APRIL SOCIAL EVENT
(Adolescent Flashback)

I got this invite, one warm spring night,
Though this time I had to wonder,
That I no longer care, who ends up with Claire,
And I'm not going to add to this blunder.

I'm sure there will Sprite, which will cause such a delight,
That's not even worthy of a mention,
Still, Billy's fat lies no longer give me a rise,
And I don't want to serve another detention.

But have each other's back, though I'll be in the rack,
I've done enough harm to my name,
And to me it's not fun, in starting trouble with Dunn,
Yet I always seem to shoulder the blame.

But don't sing the blues, try to stay off the news,
Don't screw up your futures in college,
Don't treat the girls like tramps, nor knock over more lamps,
Why waste this private school knowledge?

Still, I must hesitate, to join you on this date,
I'm depressed and not feeling really cute,
Because my date to Prom dance, won't give me a chance,
But she was nice when giving me the boot.

I hope you behave, and not make this a rave,
Or at least leave your keys at the door,
And I hope you at least think, before having a drink,
It's not cool ending up on the floor.

I'll now bid you goodbye, because I'm faking pink eye,
Though dad doesn't seem to feel sorrow,

Cause since I'm under his roof, instead of acting like a goof,
The principal won't be calling here tomorrow.

Good night and BE SAFE!

PROM NOTES

There they come – all primped and preened, hair and nailed, spit and polished. Moms are holding their kids' cellphones while the youth take selfies, the girls comment on how uncomfortable their shoes are and that maybe sometimes it'd be easier to be a guy. Parents play their roles – their oh so many roles – but you can see and feel their pride in what's going on.

As you stand and watch, you're not sure who's more stressed, though, the elders or the kids. Sure, the kids are amped times pumped times over-energized, but the parents are acting as photographers, purse, and coat holders, and they are excited and praying at the same time.

After all, didn't your mother wait up for you on Prom Night? And what time did you get home?

You laugh as you remember – the A-to-Z of Prom starting with 'Trying to Find a Date', which went with 'Not Being too Eager in Asking too Early', offset by 'Don't Wait too Late or the Good Ones will be Taken'. Then the planning and the dreaded trying on the tux. The trying to figure out how to put it on. And what exactly is or was a cumber bund? And, of course, where to store all the "Sprites."

And how are you and your gang not going to get caught?

And a present moment funny thought: Can you get a powerful hangover just from a memory?

Your laughter is interrupted by someone wanting you in their picture. A good thing – as laughing alone can draw stares, get people pointing and looking in your direction.

You know this from experience. But wait. Watch.

The buses are lined up outside, ready to tow the juniors and seniors out into the unsuspecting world. There are microphones set up for Senior Walk, and red carpet (literally). Teachers are toting scripts; some alums are back watching little brother or sister do what they remember doing.

You hope they remember better than you do – and without the headache.

You hug an alum – one of your former runners – and you smile because the fact that she wanted to come say hello to you says so much more than your won/lost record as a coach, your wearing a ring or not, and banners in the gym in this case be damned.

"I'll see you at all these senior thingies," she says. With that she's off. Brother needs a picture, mom needs about 17, dad holds the coats in this case. You wave, watch, pose, repeat. You touch the red carpet with your foot just to say you did.

You wonder where this school year went. One morning you're contemplating making all this into a book. Now it's all ending and it reminds you of a quote from one of your former tennis players, back when you were disguised as a coach of that sport. "Whatever happened to the days when it took a year for a year to go by."

Exactly. Well said. Spot on.

"Mom, what did you do with my purse?" "Where's my date?" "Did I rip this dress?" "Can we do a picture over there, in front of that sign?" "I thought you were going to ask her, what happened?"

You're swarmed by this energy – a piece of paper caught in a windstorm if you will, and you can almost swear your hair flies off with them as they go past.

And then, for a moment, you become like mom. Like dad. You envy them yet worry yet pray yet hope yet get nervous. All at once. Why? Because they're perhaps SO much like you were, and a part of you still is. This both gives you pride and scares the hell out of you at the EXACT same time.

You laugh again, reminding yourself not to do that when you're alone anymore.

Still, in a way, you too have a reason to be proud. No, they're not your kids, you'd spoil your kid so rotten he or she'd probably end up on the news. Regardless, just like your mother and father before you, you were there. You are there.

Thick and thin. Better and worse. Prom or study hall.

And you don't even have to sleep on the couch unless you want to.

Good night and be safe. PLEASE be safe…

THE ART OF TAKING AN EXAM
(Adolescent Flashback)

There she comes...the teacher...and in her hands are stacks of tests so thick they'd make a hole in the floor if she drops them. She's two rows over but she's getting closer – and though a part of you wishes an earthquake would hit, therefore postponing all this, that would only make you miserable for another day, and perhaps another.

You do what you always do in this situation – you panic, on a scale that rises with each approaching teacher's step. As she gets to your row, the mind travels, to remembering you started the semester calculating how high you could make to keep your 'A' – and now to how low you can make and not slip under your 'C'.

Forty-seven is the number, though given a curve, that can be dropped to a 36. Maybe less.

A bit of sadness mixes in with panic – your once dreams of going to an Ivy League school now reduced with your chances of even getting into...well...nowhere. Highrise condo life gives way to living under a bridge, you picture your future of begging for soup for breakfast and lunch and eating dirt for dinner.

You'd sleep next to Wendy's sacks, candy bar wrappers, and a plant, with no mail slot to hold all your Christmas cards. If any were sent.

You awaken as the offending test is plopped onto your desk. Though only words and numbers exist on there, your anxiety tells you it's your whole life, with perhaps the saddest thing that of disappointing your sweet mother.

You begin on what seems to be the first of a zillion

pages, your sweat is already on the page before any of the answers are. Still, you do the only thing an over-assigned high school kid can do:

You take out your proverbial #2 pencil and you begin:

Discuss the industrial revolution – in detail. What were the after effects of the Boston Tea Party? How did this come about?

Taking some deep breaths, you return to what you were taught: Start at the beginning, go with your first instinct. First instinct! Of a high school kid? Wow, whoever wrote these sayings were on crack, times steroids, with a touch of the above plants you'd soon be sleeping next to.

Regardless, the entire class is quiet, the teacher appears to be in "catch you cheating" position at the front. Arms folded. Glasses perched upon her nose. Eyes glaring, piercing, waiting...

The test is multiple choice, though the answers of "who cares" and "do I really need to know this" do not exist. Sweating still, you gaze around the room.

Jolene's sitting next to you, she's a smart one – has perhaps read books not written yet, and even though we're still underclassmen, she's probably already chosen her college, her first home, what to name her first two kids. Husband to be named later.

Tests for her are like physicals at a young age – a mild nuisance, nothing to be concerned over. You calculate how much you love and hate her at the exact same time.

Don's on the other side, and he would be the most likely to join you under the bridge. Once upon a time, in fact, in first grade you were asked to stick your nose in a circle on the blackboard after talking out of turn. After the teacher stuffed your face in the punishment-intended circle, she then yelled to the rest of the class, "Now does anybody want to join him?" it was none other than Don who raised his hand and said, "I do, I do!"

If there's ever a movie made about friendship, may they include that story. In fact, you laugh, though your timing is worse than bad, as not one of the test takers join you, especially including the teacher. Her "Shhh!" pounds into your ears like an alarm clock noise – said alarm set on somewhere between "jolt" and 'scare."

Anyway, after the multiple choice comes the essay answers, and you've come to almost like them and for a reason. When speaking to an adult, they can always detect your B.S. and they always interrupt you as they do so.

In writing, you can let it fly – and with each word written you have at least a chance of getting something right. At least you hope.

Moving on, Jolene's turned her test in before you even had to temptation to cheat off her paper. Harold over there has given up, his study habits rival your very own. All you hear are pencils scribbling, the clock in front ticking off seconds.

You come back to attention, some question about Hitler. You're not exactly a history buff and, again, you don't want to offend your sweet mother, but wasn't he sort of an a**hole? You make a note to take art next semester, save history for another time. Or date.

Then again, times and dates are why you want out in the first place, so painting pictures and sculpting statues are sounding better with each second.

"Time!" the teacher calls and she seems happy about this, making you think that her joy is tied to her firmness, her sense of worth. You wonder about her; what happened that made her this way?

Regardless, time means time, so you straighten your novel of a test, wonder briefly if you can refuse to put your name on it – or perhaps put someone else's – and you turn it in.

The bell rings – and you purposely avoid the part where the kids all gather in the hall to discuss what was #4 and what did you put for #7? And what was that short essay about and where were we supposed to go with that one?

You don't care. You've just went through living under bridges, putting noses in chalkboards, loving, and hating your classmates, eating dirt. Permanent records, your mother's sad face, the red ink that will soon bleed all over your poor paper. Ivy League to Podunk to better or worse or somewhere in between.

Enough for now. Onward. After all, you have English class to get to…and at least you don't have a test coming up, or at least you don't think you do…

"C" you later…

THE. LAST. DAY. OF. SCHOOL.

There's enough energy in these halls to fuel a rocket . . . past oblivion.

Think of this way: You're on your honeymoon, your lovely significant other and yourself have crossed the proverbial threshold. Zero of the thoughts from either party will be printed here, as you two approach each other. But then, suddenly, a big pane of plexiglass slides down between you, keeping you apart.

Oh, the frustration! After all, she's right there. Just right there! And you're here, inches apart. But it might as well be a mile.

That's the best way I can compare it – and because of the energy.

In fact, once upon a time while disguised as a college student, one of my friends told me before we hit the town that he was either going to "get with a woman or get into a fight." This confused me, still does unless the moon's tilted right.

To me, that's the equivalent of comparing relaxing in a soothing hot tub overlooking a scenic ocean or banging my head against a wall until my nose breaks and my teeth fall out. Curious, I had to ask.

"It's the energy, dude. It's the energy!"

Now I get it. I think.

Anyway, you're not an administrator on the last day of school, you are a jailor, period, as within 24 hours – perhaps particularly at a private school - many of these youth will be in foreign countries, lying on beaches, collecting sun, while their alarm clocks are set for August.

During the year you joke that your two rules of class are to first, not let anyone jump out the window, and second, don't let any exotic animals in the classroom. On this day, that's perhaps not so far-fetched.

The trick is to not let any of them end up on the news.

On this day, two are trying to learn guitar and, from the sound of things, not very successfully. Four more are playing poker, each pot doesn't require money though the winner appears to have a license for trash talk. One sleeps, though the word "quietly" doesn't exist around him.

And though not certain how this comes about, but on the last day at our school there is, for reasons unknown, a surplus of food. Doughnuts in this lounge or that one. Brownies in Stem Building. Banana bread in Humanities.

Maybe it's because all the refrigerators must be cleaned, renewed, wiped – old crust removed to get ready for more come August.

It's perhaps a hard-to-explain day, as the energy is everywhere but it has to be because the day goes forever. February's have come and gone in shorter time, Super Bowls with all the commercials and halftimes and replays.

And music. The last day is a license for music. And music among our youth is now the presence of every and all color and emotion – no genre is unheard. At one point, you had to stop – got some chills – as somehow, some way, Captain Fantastic and the Brown Dirt Cowboy by none other than Elton John, circa 1975, came from one of the classrooms.

Your goosebumps got to the door three steps before you did. The teacher, an older gentleman like yourself, had it going on the Smart Board. Meal Ticket. Someone Saved My Life Tonight. Curtains.

It brought back memories of losing tennis matches,

traveling across Georgia with a road map, a bag full of tennis rackets, and 8-track tape player spitting out the tunes while I-75 blended into I-16, which ran forever until you hit Savannah. The years when detours weren't a distraction but more the norm, and the days when you were discovering what and who girls were, and arrogant enough to think you could figure them out.

You laugh now at that one, though at least you're now smart enough to know that some questions don't require answers, that there are some things the male minds aren't supposed to understand. Let God work out the details, he started all this anyway.

Still, priceless times – win, lose, draw, and rain outs.

Back to the school day: It ends in the quad and it ends with the seniors. More music. Louder this time. The seniors come together in a cluster, the same way they dance nowadays. It's not 137 kids, it's one clump – a hyperactive, energetic clump.

They had just taken a victory lap – went through the hallowed halls where they had been chastised for noise all the years prior; they ran this time through those halls where they'd always been ordered to walk; yelled and hollered after years upon years upon being told to keep it down.

You stand back with the other adults, no one saying a word.

And you watch the spectators watch – the moms, dads, underclassmen. You feel them remember, see the moms cry.

The connections – the seniors – are now at center stage and the noise is fever pitch. Still, soon they will soon part, only to move off to college to form even bigger puppy huddles, and perhaps more Rated R agendas at times.

For now, though, you see the bond, put it with the music playing, watch how it makes no difference whether it fits or not.

Maybe it's this: You read once where, when angels sing, there's no such thing as it being off key. It's joyful regardless, all different yet contributing to the same.

You envy them, yet a part of you doesn't. You want to join them in college, yet you're lucky you lived through it the first time. You want to warn them and help them but this is as good a time as any to realize you can only do so much.

Sometimes, whether a teacher, parent, or coach, all you can do is stand back. And remember that often knowing when to shut up is just as, or even more important, than knowing what to say.

So, with this scene before you, with teenage adolescents at a fever pitch, you laugh silently to yourself. And as you walk away, you stop and look back one last time.

And you just stand there for a while and you watch…

A NON-VALEDICTORY ADDRESS

Graduation Day. May. Hot, a little too much so. Parents and loved ones seeking shade, some standing under the shelter given off from the Humanities Building. You can see one looking out the window from the library, the absolutely perfect "escape from long-winded speaker position" if you will.

Nice, you think. Brilliant.

Right click. Add to dictionary.

You are also in escape position. In back, off to the side, needing to "go to the restroom" like the kids have just successfully pulled off for the last 180 school days. And more to follow. One hundred, thirty-seven kids sit in the front - filled with piss and vinegar, who will live forever, who's agendas pile higher in a 30-second stretch than recipes on an eight-layer cake.

Still, as it comes to pass, you walk behind the stage for a second, look out, peer behind the podium, all those chairs and people and cameras and cellphones. Programs used for fans. Kids who won't sit still and you totally get where they're coming from.

Still, you look out.

At a view to a thrill.

You remember the speaker at your graduation – she wanted you to go join the Peace Corp. She was passionate, yet boring – two things you swore never went together – and you slept so hard while she spoke someone had to wake you before you drowned in your own drool.

You smile at the memory, though you still contend that long-winded speakers should be shot, on the spot, not subject to penalty. Like people who clog up a buffet line talking. And those people at that restaurant one night who turned off college football games to instead put on a mixed martial arts fight on every single TV! But I digress.

Getting back to the subject, life's about movement and you can see it in these kids eyes, you can read into their souls. Forced to put away their cell phones, they relax best they can, places to go, things to see, girls they can't wait to give the opportunity to reject them.

Anyway, and eventually, you join that man in the library, and you dream of what you'd wished you'd heard some 40-plus years ago…

The Speech I Needed to Hear

In this world, where it's almost mandatory you grow up too fast, buy this or that to look the part, network here, send off a resume there, slow down! It's all non-stop. The lessons are "Hurry! Get the degree, the wife or husband! Buy the house, have the 2.3 kids. Lock your doors. Insure things. Have your lawyer, accountant, and bosses numbers on speed dial."

Before long, you're more scattered, smothered, and covered than a Waffle House order – you're checking the outer boxes but you've forgotten your inner soul. You're taught – even since kindergarten for crying out loud – how to work for somebody.

Uses time well. Gets along with others. Promptness. More boxes, more grades, move along these lines which lead to….

Where exactly?

Try this if you will. Find your soul. Sit quietly in a room alone. And instead of what you could do that makes you the most money, what would you do for free? Funny thing – God works that way – that's probably the thing that will check the 'money' box.

What are you doing when time flies, you forget to eat, and you've forgotten to turn the oven off and your turkey is now so burnt and hard you could fight off a tribe of Ninjas if they broke down your door.

Funny again – being yourself is the hardest thing there is – more so than Algebra and logarithms put together.

A memory, for what it's worth: I'm in college, in my dorm, inspired by four shots of tequila, two upcoming tests, and one broken heart. It was there that I discovered the meaning of life but, not knowing I liked to write, forgot to record it – couldn't remember it for the life of me and I stumble to this day, to my watering hole in hopes of recalling what I'd forgotten, digging up something long buried.

But I called her, told her how great she was, no hard feelings. My best friend, upon hearing this, immediately scolded me for my dumbassery (oops, right click, add to dictionary again. I know that's not a word, but I've created it, just for that occasion. With all apologies to my good English teachers out there).

Later, I felt really good, and not from all I'd just embalmed myself with. Caring and appreciation and – without getting too touchy-feely, love – are all natural things. Not normal, but natural. It's the closest to God we'll ever get – and maybe that's part of what I forgot to write down.

Anyway, I laughed. Said object of my affection right outside my window, off to marry someone with all the boxes checked. And me just wanting a bed and a book and a burrito. At the time, I just needed something that would put me peacefully to sleep – like a novel written in Latin.

Use your 20's for trial and error! Try this. Try that. If and when all else fails, go back to grad school. Start over. Go to concerts. Go through the rites of passages of life: wait tables, officiate some sporting event, get dumped. Walk a girl to the door, try to kiss her, only to have her turn her head and you kiss her on the ear. Laugh, cry, scream, throw things, hang out with friends.

Wash. Rinse. Repeat.

When you hit 30, you should start by now to feel what your soul is telling you to do. Not the whole picture - you say you want that but you don't. After all, when you sit down to eat, do you want every meal ever for the rest of your life?

No. Dr. Martin Luther King said it best: "You don't have to see the whole staircase, just take the first step."

Then follow the bouncing ball. Connect the dots. And they're everywhere, though unfortunately drowned out by too much information. And turn off the news! There will ALL-WAYS (one word and two) be something you're supposed to be scared about.

Shortages. Inflation. Gas prices. Wars. Stock Market. Running out of milk when you still have more cereal. Stitches and doctor reports and flat tires, oh my!

The world thrives on motivating you with fear, though ironically, you're filled with love. It's like college if you think about it: guys hit their sexual peak while there, girls later at around 35. Why is this, you ask? Because God likes to laugh, too, and if both peaks hit simultaneously, Dr. Thompson would've gone off to give his Econ lecture and nobody would've been there.

Regardless, I like to believe there's a perfect accounting

behind all this chaos. Order among debris, an inner light while you stumble through darkness.

Still, if I had to give advice for going to college, I have two things to tell the girls, something similar to the guys. For you girls, first off, beware of "needy" guys at parties – there will be plenty, and number two, if you can handle distractions when you need to – there will also be plenty – you'll be fine.

As for the guys, Rule 2 applies to you, and as for Rule 1, be respectful. In all due respect to Mr. Shakespeare, words CAN hurt, but they can also help, perhaps move the world in the right direction. After all, there will be times when you need to persuade people, whether verbally or with the written word. Like applying to college or for a job. Or more importantly, when trying to woo a woman.

And maybe even most important: when you're trying to talk your way out of trouble with the woman you've already wooed!

Go outward, but never forget to look inward. A writer once told me that you had to have the bricks before you can build the house. With that said, forget the house for now, go collect the bricks. Good ones. Bad. Rotten. Faded. Jaded. Perfect. Fitting. Horrible.

Find the bricks, the flow, and then toss in some seeds of your own.

Contribute with you and what you are. Make your personality your job. And nervousness? You'll be scared shitless often but, when all is said and done, if you love what you do, and love the people you do it with the best you can, then all else will take care of itself.

After all, unless you're working for NASA or some-where, most of life isn't an exact science, so just take it on the fly, a bit here, a little there.

Find your passion and work it, but don't forget to take the days with the top down, your spirits up, a map leading to who cares, agendas thrown into the shredder.

After all, if you love life, life will love you back.

So, love as much as you can and give gratitude at every turn. But don't forget to include yourself when you're throwing all these emotions out.

Congratulations! And for God sakes, keep your headphones off as much as possible. You're connecting to a lot when you're staring at those things, but you're missing so much more.

So much more.

God's Love, and always listen to that feeling in your gut…

Because ironically, we all look up when praying, but a piece of God is located within – somewhere between your gut and your heart.

And when all is said and done, whether through the worse or through the best, just listen.…

AN UNNATURAL SILENCE

It'd make a great scene from a scary movie – walking down a high school hallway so quiet you can hear the sound of your creaking footsteps. After all, the school year hath ended.

No kids to step over; nary a one on the floor encircled by books and cellphones and friends. Nobody coming towards you, imparting gossip or agendas or nothing at all. No one preoccupied, nor is there another filled with adrenaline and looking for someone to spill it upon.

Still, the mental noise makes up for it, as just yesterday this very walk was crowded by balloons and food and games and toys. A last day doesn't come and go quietly into that good night – it kicks and screams with exclamation points, louder and longer than the morning announcements, follows you into this class and that.

The last day of classes you sit among Bored Energy if that makes sense. The other 179 days you may be a teacher, the last day you are their jailor. The clock on the wall, once only ticking towards yet another day of school, now stands in the way of beach houses, penthouses, boat houses, and the like.

And there aren't enough cheerleaders in the world that can clap and yell it forward fast enough.

You sit feeling guilty for the most part, because the laws say they must stay until the allotted time. You feel their pain, you share it, actually, because not only have you been there, but there will always be a part of you that is still there.

Yes, the body can grow old, but the mind doesn't have to. I know this as a bi-lingual man – I speak English but I'm also very fluent in High School.

It's ironic – how I hear parents say how these kids just

DO NOT LISTEN! I'm here to defend and tell you that they do – the problem is that there are just SO many people and SO many things going on that it's tough for an adolescent mind to take it all in.

It's the Universal Vacuum Law of High Schools, which states that in order to let some things in, then other things must be left out. And that's where the parents come in and there's where they often lose.

It's not personal… It really isn't.

I'm reading their little minds as I walk in this physical silence among this mental hyperactivity. "Turn your lacrosse uniform in." "Your final drafts must be turned in by 11:59!" "We're hanging out at John's tonight. Bring your swimsuit because you're going to get thrown in anyway."

"Don't forget to pick up your brothers' flute at the front desk. He has a concert." "You left your room a mess." "Track your miles this summer and send them in. Cross country practice will be here soon."

I couldn't do it – be a high school kid again I mean. It's sensory overload, testing overload, sports overload, just plain out overload. I feel this now as I walk, I still here and feel the stress and the tests, the pain and the gain, the tears and the fears.

As I stop at the end, I try to silence the lambs if you will. Still, this youth has made me bi-lingual of tongue and more so of the soul. I cried tears of joy twice only seven days ago. Sat last night on a couch too tired to make the seven yard trek to my bed.

In the midst of all this, in spite of all this, because of all this, and as much as I like to write about my sweet mother, it is the words of my father that push all this – so much of this – out of the way – as I head back to my desk.

"Keep it coming…."

And have a great summer…

A LETTER TO MY TEACHERS I SHOULD'VE ALREADY WRITTEN

I remember sitting at high school graduation – I did graduate without honors for what it's worth though nobody cares, including me at the time. For the record, there were 22 in our class and I was number 21.

Let's just say I wasn't surprised when I wasn't named the Valedictorian and let's move on.

Before I thank my teachers about 50 years too late, first this:

French came mostly normal while logarithms remain foreign. History is history so I didn't at the time understand why we bothered, science involved slimy things and cutting up that poor frog. Speaking of that day, I will neither confirm nor deny that incident with Claire Smith involving utensils, let's just chalk that up as boys being boys and move on, okay?

Psychology intrigued me, art had hot girls in there so I signed up, and study hall was for passing notes, throwing things, and taking naps. Seeing a teacher in the halls usually resulted in me running the other way; I later became a marathon runner so you do the math.

Still, again years later, I looked up the word 'educate' and what I read astounded me. After all, it's the art of "drawing out of, NOT putting into." I love this, because I remember the day my English teacher read an essay by Edgar Allan Poe. Poe was wacked, mostly insane, and often a mentally tortured writer. In short, I immediately loved him, and his quote about "going insane with horrible periods of sanity" ranks beautiful in my ears to this very day.

Anyway, when my friend Ken tried to talk to me

during the reading, I told him to "shut the (bleep) up," and I can assure you there wasn't enough soap in that Madison, Georgia town to wash out my dirty mouth.

Still.... that 'drawing out from' thing.

And before I close with that, I never knew how the words and actions of kids could make or break your day. With that said, I'm not here to congratulate you on your subject knowledge, but mostly – and perhaps all the way – on your ability to give a damn (oops, more soap) plain out, day after day, year after year, class after class.

After all, knowledge can be simply information, it rings in some ears and gets rejected like an NBA blocked shot in others.

Regardless, trying to contain the uncontainable every day and living and dying as to the result. Going home frustrated, wondering, pondering, tweaking, and re-tweaking in respect to a population where some will get it and some won't.

In moving on, I'm not really sure what my view is on this Judgment Day thing we read about in the Bible, but I won't bore you with my weirdness. If there is one, I think that in the long line waiting to get into Heaven, the teachers can simply walk through, unchecked.

No I.D. cards required, no dress code, and I wish that bouncer at the Limelight years ago had that attitude but that's another story.

Regardless, I also think that God, while judging all the others, will take the time to give each of you a smile as you go past.

My mother was a teacher, and I'd like to know that God beamed brightly as that Southern Belle walked across, and I laugh knowing she returned the gesture while going forward to continue correcting my father.

But that, again, is another story.

In moving on, I'm sorry that I ruined a lot of days. I didn't realize that teaching is the most challenging and difficult thing there is. Weathermen, for example, can make lots of money being wrong and the results will be what the results will be.

But your results move forward – in all shapes, forms, and sizes. Your voices, regardless of the adventures ahead, will peck their way into souls at odd times – will nudge people while they sleep.

So, thank you is my long-winded point. Mom, tell dad I forgive him for stealing my bedroom and turning into a messy art studio. Claire, I contend that that was your fault – I wasn't sure what girls were yet and I'm still not sure I do now, either.

And finally, I've learned that the greatest prayer ever given is only two words: Thank you.

And now, perhaps too late but I'd like to think better late than never, I'll give you those two words.

And I couldn't mean it more.

SUMMER PLANS

- "Any beach. Anywhere. Really don't care."
- "I'm going to kiss at least four girls. Last summer I kissed five, but then I got slapped. That takes away two – house rules."
- "Summer? Thanks to APUSH I've got summer school!"
- "Will I get demerits if I tell you what I'm doing?"
- "I'm going to hide from my mom because she, like, makes me clean my room and stuff."
- "For the record, I'm going to do whatever I undertake to the best of my ability. Off the record...well...I'm not going to tell you."
- "Are you going to print this?"
- "I was bargaining for the Bahamas but then I got grounded. So, I guess it's Panama City or Myrtle Beach. Something like that."
- "Not sure but will I have to write an essay on it when I get back? Because I, like, hate writing essays during school enough as it is."
- "Sleep a lot, sprinkled among some naps. Oh, and I'll rest and take it easy, too."
- "The family vacation of course. It used to be fun but sometimes it can be sort of lame. I mean, I've got younger brothers."
- "I'm going to try waiting tables again. I have experience, though that may not help since I got fired. I shouldn't put that on my application, right?"
- "We're loading up all ten horses and I'm going show jumping down in Wellington."
- "Starting a rock and roll band. We don't have any gigs yet but we don't suck. At least not too bad."

- "I have to get my miles in where I don't puke the first day of cross country practice like I did last year."
- "I'm working a summer camp in North Carolina. That way I can laugh when I'm yelling at the kids, the way you guys do when you're yelling at me."
- "My family just travels. I don't know, we just get on planes and go places."
- "Currently I'm bartering with my dad. He wants me to learn the family business. I'm trying to convince him that if he hires me, it may not be much of a business anymore."
- "We always go out west and, I've got to tell you, every year it gets harder to come back here."
- "Play a lot of video games and a lot of golf."
- "I'm going to some beach. Speaking of, can I read this book when you get through writing it?
- "Basketball camps. As if the season doesn't take up enough holidays as it is."
- "Golf! Because the coach told me this spring when he cut me that I needed to get…like…good at it."
- "Venezuela. My dad's from there though I don't know why I have to go. I mean, that's not my problem – I have enough problems here as it is."
- "I have a couch in the living room and I may never get off of it. In fact, even going to the bathroom and eating are going to be major distractions."
- "I'm going to try to get in the Guinness Book of Records. Did you know that if you throw a ping pong ball into a paper cup from 35 feet away, then you're in?"
- "Fight with my sister. My parents told me to get good at something, right?"

- "I'm going to take up a new sport - one that doesn't hurt if I screw up. I did this last year, though boxing didn't turn out to be the best solution."
- "Visiting colleges, can you believe that? I get out of this school and my parents want me to go look at bigger ones! What a world!"
- "Same things I did last summer except this time I hope I don't get caught."
- "We're renovating my room. Not sure, but this might be a hint of some kind."

Closing bell thoughts: *Listening to the above answers, it's a wonder we all don't catch every disease on the planet when they get back from all this and gather in the same buildings. COVID could be the least of it.*

Still, I wish them luck on their trips to boat houses, lake houses, penthouses, and beach houses. As for me, I'll try and stay clear of the outhouses.

Happy travels. Happy tanning. Stay out of trouble. Will miss you all.

But I'm going to sleep. And I don't care what time it is.

AFTERWORD

My own thoughts after a year in the halls:

- I want to come back in another life as some of these kids.
- There's no way in hell I want to be one of these kids.
- Finishing a book feels great!
- Finishing a book is depressing! What now?
- It's summer – the energy's gone like the air out of a balloon.
- I must find another project before I develop more bad habits. Like that COVID year.
- I hope this book made you laugh, think, and cry.
- May you learn to live and love the way dog's do.
- Except may you live longer.
- I hope you have a place you can go in the morning where you can just sit, ponder, contemplate, and get your (bleep) together before starting your day.
- If your son ever falls through the roof of his school – and I'm still not sure how that happened – may you go easy on him. (Putting this in here for a friend).
- May you learn it's not complicated – put good out, get good back.
- May your dog be potty trained before he ruins your good rug – and chews up all your ink pens.
- Because waiting until he runs out of ink can be messy – and seemingly eternal.
- May you find your own version of hallways – a

place where you're supported, through good times and in bad.

- May you never get burned by a pair of aces after you've thrown down a pair of kings.
- May you learn to take all your experiences, relationships, and situations, and learn the art of letting go, forgiving, and translating it all into love and peace.
- When in doubt, may you write down, then return to when and what you were doing that made you happiest – then find a way to create or recreate that.
- May you never start a night with Jägermeister because it won't end well. And you won't remember it even if it did.
- Call her. And may you always have more guts than I've shown when doing so.
- When sitting at a Vegas crap table, only take as much money as you'd spend on a night out. After all, the place wasn't created from people winning.
- Don't ever argue over who was better – the Beatles or the Rolling Stones. After all, you can't prove it. Then again, who really cares if you could?
- Whether succeeding or failing in a relationship or a sporting contest, win or lose with class. After all, anyone can be happy when they're winning. What's that prove?
- May all our kids – and yours – be safe over these things called summers, and may they not take for granted they get these freedoms to begin with.
- Then again, I think they deserve it.
- A friend is as a friend does. Just because someone will have a drink with you, that doesn't mean squat. They might just be thirsty. Or an alcoholic. Perhaps both.

- In the random Super Bowl betting games, bet the over on how long the National Anthem's going to last. Singers like to extend that last note at the end – once it lasted longer than my high school Latin class.
- Just do it. Then again, not always.
- And thanks! Always thanks. It's one of the best words you can ever think or say.

Dunn Neugebauer
February 2023

ABOUT THE AUTHOR

Dunn Neugebauer lives in Atlanta where he works at a school – serving in the communication department, coaching both cross country and track, subbing in the Upper School, announcing home football games, and working carpool. He has written for many newspapers, some of which include the Northside Neighbor, The Tampa Tribune, The St. Pete Times, Palm Beach Post, and others, while also penning columns in magazines and a blog that appears on Facebook four-to-six times per week.

Growing up, he attempted many sports, though later moved on to play collegiate tennis. As a coach, he has been a part of two recent state championship teams – one in girls' cross country and the other in boys' track. He takes no full credit for either, but instead simply enjoys being "the Coral Reefer Band to a lot of Jimmy Buffets."

When not doing all of the above, he can be found jogging at the river (slowly), starting each morning at Dunkin Donuts, and often sitting in the library at his school gazing out into the world at nothing in particular.

He lives alone, though often shares his condo with guests, house keepers, and more often than not, his pet roach. This is actually his seventh book, though his novel he penned in 1996 he doesn't like to talk about, as he was "just practicing" at the time.

Regardless, he is forever grateful for his readers as "they bring joy to what can often be a lonely profession."